A
LETTER
to
MY SON

A memoir

A LETTER *to* MY SON

A memoir

TAHSINUR CHOWDHURY

EDITED BY FAHAD ALAM E

gatekeeper press™
Tampa, Florida

A LETTER TO MY SON:
A Memoir

Published by Gatekeeper Press
7853 Gunn Hwy, Suite 209
Tampa, FL 33626
www.GatekeeperPress.com

Cover image from: iStockphoto.com/acilo

Library of Congress Control Number: 2023940001

ISBN (paperback): 9781662939723
eISBN: 9781662939730

To my beloved mother,
Taj-n-Nehar Chowdhury

CONTENTS

Dear son,

Legacy... There is something about humans and their actions to go to lengths just to say, "I was here!'" Our mortal persons are so invested and obsessed with the ties of this world that we yearn for remembrance. We find comfort in knowing that some part of us would be present—even after time compels us to bite the dust—in some shape or form, in practices, in principles, in ideas, in memories or memoirs like this one. Somehow, the idea of going down without a last shot, the idea of losing to life and to time unsettles us. Hence, a yearning of leaving a mark is born; leaving a souvenir for our fellow men is probably how we all prepare (or would like to) for the inevitable.

My son, do not interpret the words of your father as a desperate attempt at clinging on. On the contrary, this is your father trying to outsmart life and the ever-punctual ticking of time; for at least once, I want to plan and succeed. Age and solitude make one think of many things; after all, it can only be helped for so long! I reckon these thoughts keep chasing you all your youth. When you slow down (without your consent), when you do not have to race life and would rather just sit down and watch others do so in vain, these thoughts finally catch up to you. Age often begets wisdom, and wisdom begets regrets. I am sure that I did my best in my younger days and yet, somehow, I am sitting here thinking that I could have probably done more. No, I could have done more! I am met with the conclusion that I could have shared so much more with you and Aneesa for that probably would have opened up the avenue in turn for both of you to share more with me. Remember when you were both so young and would with such mad exhilaration broadcast every detail of your day? With time and with our failure to meet your level of energy and excitement, those instances have just faded away as if they were never there.

With you and Aneesa now out to college, I just feel... lonely. It is so clichéd that I feel strange even saying it aloud or writing it out. I guess admission of weakness seldom gets realized by our insecurities.

The house's silent space in your absence renders me nostalgic and reminiscent of my past: a time before both of you came into my life; a time of stepping into the shoes of fatherhood; a time that shapes a boy into a man and a girl into a woman.

Humans are curiously predictable; we rarely break off from our routines, our brain likes being lazy. There was a time when you used to depend on me... for everything. I remember the nights when it was my turn to "keep watch" like it was yesterday. When I was wide awake, ready to take on any "challenge" you would throw at me, on high alert, on my toes, both of you, on the other hand, would sleep peacefully—not a peep! It was almost promptly after I let my guard down and indulged in an unconscious nap that the world would start to fall apart. It was Aneesa with the need for someone by her side and, when she had grown up, it was you demanding a diaper change in the most unlikely night hours. But then again, no hour is "unlikely" during that phase of parenthood. They say it takes a community to raise a child. I guess I was performing the duties of a whole community on those nights during two different periods of my life (not that I did not have the occasional assistance). I will tell you, as curiously predictable as we are, my first experience with early parenthood did not remotely season me enough for my second one. Even then, I felt like I was freshly embarking on the journey of parenthood again as if I were starting all over. Not that I am complaining; I would do it again in a heartbeat, knowing I might feel like a father who learned very little from his first two attempts! I cannot help but chuckle now! I wonder if that is how every parent feels about taking care of their babies. Is that how my mother felt too?

I have had similar experiences with you both and yet how differently you both have turned out. It is amazing. What I miss most are your childhood days; I miss them just as much as I miss my childhood. From the day you were born, I took care of you, kept you clean and dry, walked you, drove you to school, bathed you, fixed your favorite meals—your broccoli and Aneesa's golden fried eggplant—and put you to bed... And how can I forget the sand in your shoes! There was always a ton of sand that needed to be emptied off your shoes after school. Every experience I learned something about both of you: names of your first friends on your first day in kindergarten; about your first skirmish (learned from your teacher of course!); your favorite subjects; all the ingenious excuses you came up with to avoid your most loathed vegetables; the different tastes and preferences you both grew for bedtime stories. Nothing cements moments into memories like time.

I know how people like things to be concise these days and you must excuse me for this will not exactly be a short letter. I will, however, make it worth your time. Aneesa and you will appreciate this letter—not today but later on, years from now when you are a little older, have your kids, and I will be long gone. One winter night when snow will be gently touching the ground and one late Blue Jay will be in a hurry to leave, this letter will find you ... Open it! You will remember me.

MY MOTHER'S WISHES

I have fond memories of my childhood, and they seem to be fond of me as well. No wonder these moments keep sneaking into my subconscious mind once in a while. I automatically give in to the temptation, no struggle involved; none is necessary. My eyes close softly and I immediately find myself in the land of reminiscence.

Bogulagari, a village near Jaldhaka in Bangladesh—my village—where it all began... The entrance leading to the gates of my cherished memories would usually be covered with dry leaves, the fresh smell of earth, and a warm sense of belonging... of finally being home! With my eyes still shut, I cannot wait to walk in.

Familiar faces, now older than they used to be—probably a little wrinkled, probably a lot gray—also traveled through time and greeted me at the threshold. Hugs and smiles stretched from one ear to the other, we metamorphose into a band of ten-year-olds in our dusty shorts and tank tops; the whole lot—friends, cousins, nephews—lead the way and beckon me to follow. I oblige without sparing a single thought.

Our process of growing up took place beyond the boundaries, beyond the walls, of home. I grew up playing outside with my friends. And yet, amidst games and important matches, I would run back home for the most manageable reasons. It might have been too hot outside and I needed a quick drink. Or we were playing hide and seek and my house, being closest, was the safest hiding place. Or, now as I look back, I probably was a young child finding all sorts of excuses to come home just to see my mother. A glimpse would suffice, a sneak peek at my most prized treasure, away from the sight of the whole world, to make sure everything was alright. After that, I would return to my friends until it was dusk. There was something very powerful in these brief interactions that were different from the others that took place throughout the day. A mother's presence always symbolizes a sense of security and comfort. And I was no stranger to this feeling.

My father passed away when I was nine years old but my mother passed away in January 1996. Aneesa was two years old and you were yet to be born. Born in September 1996, you were eight months too late to play in your grandma's arms or coo endearingly at her, or yawn at her attempts at trying to establish communication with a newborn. She would have been thrilled to see you. Alas! Neither you nor Aneesa had the chance to know her.

"Tell your children about me. Read my letters to them." That is what she wrote in her last letter to me when I was in Missouri. She wanted Aneesa and you to know her. She wanted to be remembered.

As I said earlier, humans have an inevitable yearning for remembrance.

She also wrote,

It has been thirty-five years since your father passed away. I am the sole witness to my family's countless joys and sorrows. From British India to Bangladesh, I have seen a lot. Time blessed me with the age and fortune to see the weddings of my grandchildren! With that, I feel that I have seen my share of the world. I have this fleeting feeling that there isn't much left for me to see. However, I long to meet your daughter Aneesa. Bring her to me. I want to see her before I am called for.

Soon it was that time of the year. We were enroute to Bangladesh. As per your grandma's wishes, Aneesa accompanied us. She was two years old. We all gathered in my mother's room, around her bed—Mother on the bed and Aneesa on her lap; Mother eighty-five years old and Aneesa, a mere fraction of that number. We videotaped Aneesa and my mother; she was in her grandma's arms, cooing, smiling, and yawning. My mother's wish to meet little Aneesa was finally realized.

Both almost three generations apart, sharing no common language of communication, yet, I could tell, they read each other's eyes like routine work of centuries old. I think, as Aneesa bathed in the adoration of my mother's frail arms, they had an exchange that was nothing short of special. I am unaware of the specifics of the discourse; nevertheless, I am content with being a witness to such a rare scene prospect.

"The resemblance is uncanny!"

Whether they meant it or it was just customary to say so, I didn't know. But I sat there marveling at what seemed like half the village vouching that Aneesa was your grandmother's spitting image.

Honestly, I could not care less if they didn't mean it. They all meant well and had your grandmother's best interest at heart. You see, your grandmother was suffering from depression at the time. It had evolved into a chronic problem for her. When she was not depressed, she was full of life. She would go out, socialize, and be her old self. But then depression would envelop her and she would lose all interest in life. She would just stay in bed all day, refusing to talk, to get out of her room, or to even eat. Aneesa's presence, although for that brief instance, fixed that. My mother constantly sought out her granddaughter while we were there.

Brief it was—the stay…

Soon it was time for goodbyes. Leaving my past behind in the past, darting towards the future, we returned back to Columbia, Missouri. Two weeks into our return, on January 19, 1996, your *ammu* and I drove to Kansas City to attend our US citizenship ceremony. We took the oath along with many others from different places in the world and became US citizens. We were ecstatic to have found another home beyond home! It was a wonderful feeling. We returned home in the evening, picking Aneesa up from her babysitter on our way back. The situation called for a celebration.

There were three messages on the answering machine from our family members.

All calls were identical. All those voicemails stressed the feverish urgency to return the calls. The tone of the messages said it all. I knew what the calls were about. I sat down on the chair. My mother's picture was hanging on the wall. I looked outside through the glass door. It was snowing in Missouri...

She was admitted to a clinic. After we left for the states, her depression only got worse. She was suffering. One evening she just slipped away in her sleep, just the way she always wanted.

At 85, her long life had finally reached the finish line.

United States

It all begins with a step… with baby steps.

I am often reminded of how amazed I was when you started to crawl. It would always bring me immense pleasure to see you both slowly and cheerfully move around the house on all fours. When I was home, it became my favorite pastime: "Now, where are you off to?" I would ask you at the sight of you creeping from one room to the other. No two children are the same. I had begun to contemplate that during my early fatherhood years, almost as soon as I had you! You could only imagine how proud I was when both my children, well, failed in their attempts at their first baby steps. I would always cheer, sometimes with apparent encouragement, sometimes inwardly. I had to tread carefully to not alarm you in your ambitions and to reassure you that you were not alone. And then, like magic, you were walking and then running around. Even after the initial awe, the applause had not come to a pause because there is always something new, always something to look forward to. With every baby step, I was always entertained, always amazed!

And then, like no time had passed, you grew up! Those steps were more confident, more determined. You moved forward with purpose. I remember when I, an international student, ventured through the doors of the University of Detroit; it feels like yesterday. And now, my children are walking over my footprints, following the same steps as they go to university.

College is a wonderful place to be. I barely had a dime to spare to afford the nuances of socializing that makes college special and even though I was living hand to mouth during those years, I enjoyed campus life thoroughly. University was a window to the world and I was gawking to my heart's content. You will find it to be this unique place, a world within the world. You meet contemporaries from many countries and many cultures, and they will season your learning experience with their individuality. People, people are who make college a unique place.

The vastness of the American land is something that I still have trouble grasping. That was the first thing that hit me during my initial assessment. Miles and miles of empty land just sitting there! Coming from a densely populated Bangladesh, the comparison was instinctive but natural. I was overwhelmed by the openness of the land.

I did not initially come to Detroit; my first date with an American state was Iowa. Liza, your aunt, was living in Iowa City and I crashed at her place for few days before going to

Detroit. I remember Fairchild Street in Iowa City, the very first address I lodged in.

It was April when I came to Iowa. I woke up one afternoon from my jet lag hangover to a pleasant smell. I was about to jump down from the bed, ready to sprint for the familiarly delicious aroma that felt like home but something from the back of my mind stopped me in my course. I laid there for some time, staring at the ceiling, absorbing my new space, acclimating to it. As familiar as the smell was, my view was not one that I was accustomed to waking up to. Within a few blinks, my mind diligently reminded me of where I was. I recognized the color of the ceiling, and then I examined the walls along with the accouterments that hang on them. When all the pieces of furniture and everything else in the room were accounted for, I walked nonchalantly to the window and looked outside. The sight that lay beyond me was something I was prepared for—after all the cold flooring had signaled me what to expect—snow. It was what I realized afterward that shook me. I did not see a single soul! It was as if someone had drawn a clean, white sheet over the land and everything had gone to hibernate underneath it. The silence was eerily frightening. "Graveyards of Bangladesh are noisier than this," I remember saying to myself.

The anxiety was soon followed by calm when I recognized that it was part of the natural process. Spring is around the corner, and once again nature would shower us with her warm benevolence. Robin would once again be returning to the branches of the apple trees; she, like nature, will keep her promise and hopefully I will get to see the good citizens of Iowa make some noise. My nose was tingling; the pleasant aroma was getting stronger now. The temptation was irresistible! I followed the trail to the aroma. I found Liza at the scene, in the kitchen, having her merry way with our mother's recipe for chicken. I knew I recognized that smell.

Liza is my youngest of six sisters and yet she had such a mature aura about her. She was always a loving and caring person. I suppose she claimed most of my mother's personality! The little girl from childhood, who ran about the house with her two ponytails neatly tied with ribbons, became like a Rock of Gibraltar to me ever since I arrived in the States in my good times and bad times (especially during the bad times.) After spending a few days with Liza, I came to Detroit.

Detroit was an interesting place. The director of International Students informed us that we needed to familiarize ourselves with the basic parlance of Detroit. It was essential to go about the city, essential for survival. It was during this exchange with him that I learned how words have different meanings in different parts of the world, and different contexts. "Bad could be GOOD!" "When someone says, 'You look bad!,' it means you look good!" the director said. Over the years I got good at picking up other jargon of Detroit. "What up doe?" is one of my absolute favorites. The phrase's ability to exhibit a range of emotions, sometimes completely con-flicting ones, was baffling to me initially. But then again, that is how it works in Detroit. I suppose you only understand that range of emotions when you share with a person that level of intimacy by having the same palette of the vernacular.

I couldn't say I am keen on it but Detroit did open doors to a world of a diverse range of art and acquainted me with so many talented artists. Talking of music and artists, I was in-troduced to Motown music for the first time in Detroit-gifted musicians with wonderful music. I liked downtown Detroit, Detroit River, and Canada on the other side.

The preliminary excitement and appeal of my first visit to the States were beginning to wane as things started getting serious and university was getting ever more demanding. Of the times that I did not spend attending classes or browsing through books at the library, I was working part-time. I took up a job at the school cafeteria along with other students. And then, probably because I strained myself and worked my fingers to the bones, I hurt my back. I could hardly walk. The backache stretched down and I soon developed severe pain in my leg too.

In the conditions that I found myself in, being alone in Detroit was doing me little good so I went back to Iowa City to stay at Liza's place. Mother had come to the States to stay with her for a while. I was in pain but here I was comfort-able with my family, albeit I was on bedrest all the time. I had to go through surgery on my back at the University of Iowa Hospitals & Clinics. The whole procedure took some time but, as I was under the spell of anesthesia, I went into a deep state of sleep with the last person before my eyes being an assuring doctor who informed me that I was in good hands. When I woke up, I was greeted with encores and affection from your Aunt Liza, your Uncle Karim, and Grandma which were received with casual bravado from my end! The doctors and nurses were quite nice and I was well taken care of. Within a short period, I healed from the surgery and after some time I was so happy to walk again. To test myself, almost as if to celebrate my recovery, every afternoon I went out for walks. I used to walk miles in Iowa City with its rolling streets, lines of maple trees (Were they maple though? I am not sure), small homes with hardwood floors (at least that is what they seemed to me), all very peaceful. Iowa healed my back and my spirits. Rejuvenated and recharged, I was ready to return to Detroit and to live with roommates.

We (my roommates and I) had several landlords in Detroit but I remember Gabriel most vividly. Gabriel was a wonderful human being, always smiling. If I remember correctly, he used to play jazz—the kind of music that, I think, is played/loved by people who are content with their lives, or at least that's the kind of vibe Gabriel set. One cold winter month, he stopped by to chat as he often did. Quite casually, he whisked out our energy bill for the other month. We were billed for an amount that was more than we paid Gabriel in rent. He never complained though. He was smiling during the whole conversation while we could only apologize. We came from warm countries and the Detroit cold did not suit us well. We probably overworked the thermostat on the max dial!

Some of us international students lived close to the campus because we had no cars at the time. This made more sense for international students especially since the first few years of their lives usually revolved around the university. However, the neighborhood was not exactly trouble-free. Unpleasant revelations awaited us occasionally, if not daily. Sometimes kids from the area would break into the apartment, and "help themselves" to some of our stuff when we were not home.

One day a young man came to our door asking for me; he was holding my passport. He demanded money for returning it. That is probably how this kid got a taste for extortion! He was the kid who broke into our apartment the day earlier. How do I know, you wonder? Well, I came home to a missing briefcase and my passport happened to be in it. This gentleman took my briefcase and now was kind enough to return one of the artifacts from the briefcase, all of course in exchange for a little something for being a good and responsible "Samaritan." I was not at home to answer his plea but my roommate, Ajit, attended to him. Ajit told the kid to come back later when I would be home. But the kid never showed up. I waited with impatient anxiety but he never returned. I do not know why. He could have made ten bucks easily. I would have started with five and negotiated up. It cost me forty dollars and a few days more of impatience (and anxiety) to get a new passport. Ten dollars would have been a good barter for both of us. Maybe he thought we would inform the cops and he would find himself "rolling" in cuffs instead of rolling in cash. He should have known that we would never bother the Detroit police for such minor inconveniences. Breaking and stealing would have been considered minor inconveniences in Detroit, at least in the neighborhood where some of us lived. Back in the day, you did not call Detroit cops unless there was a body lying on the floor. You would simply be wasting their time.

A few years later when I went to the American Embassy in Bangladesh for my green card interview, the first question the officer asked me was, "Whatever happened to your original passport? Did you sell it?" I said something along the lines of, "I used to live in Detroit; losing my passport was the least of my concerns. It was my life that I tried not to lose." She issued the green card and did not ask any further questions.

We called the cops only once. It was a summer night.

David and I were in our home. David was another of my roomies and he hailed from Madras, India. He was smart, charming, and very sociable—the type who made friends easily, the type one would like to be friends with.

And naturally, owing to our shared Asian characteristics but mostly to his genial ways and his sense of humor, we clicked and soon became good friends. David made my life in Detroit a whole lot more interesting and enjoyable. That night, he announced that he was going to go to the neighborhood store. He probably wanted to buy a pack of cigarettes or something else. When he returned, I discovered him at the entrance with two guys. I greeted them with a "hello." I thought David knew them. It turned out they brought David home at gunpoint.

Before I could understand what was happening, before I was able to give in to my instinct to react, I was promptly signaled to stay quiet and make way for their entry. As soon as they were inside, one of them pushed David onto me and pointed their guns toward the interior of the house. The language between that of an intruder and that of a victim is as universal as fear. Paralyzed by this very medium of communication and our senses focused on doing whatever was necessary for survival, we did as we were told. Our bodies moved on their own first, and our brains processed the demands of intruders later. We were escorted into the bedroom and our hands were then tied behind our backs and to the bed. A robbery was in progress. Everything happened like clockwork, so fast.

They were probably professionals in this line of business, individuals who knew their roles well—two individuals who knew the part of "good robber/bad robber" down to the T.

That is how it seemed then! One of them, brandishing his gun aggressively, constantly threatened to kill us while the other kept repeating "Don't kill them!" a sort of mantra to calm someone who seemed somewhat trigger-happy. Maybe he was a regular guy who appeared as Death personified to a couple of boys who have never experienced such fear in their pasts. The objective of their conflicting roles!? Keeping us confused and scared, and manipulating us into complete cooperation.

I was not sure if they were serious about killing us. Initially, I thought this would be a simple robbery, that maybe they were trying to scare us into submission. This was, again, unnecessary since we were already frightened to bits and voluntarily cooperative. Two against two and a gun. We were outnumbered. This was no time for heroics! David kept telling me to stay cool, and I kept thinking about my mother. I knew if something were to happen to me, she would be living in grief for the rest of her life. I did not want to be the cause of her sorrow. I, in turn, kept urging David to calm down. The whole space was filled with a cacophony of voices filled with anger, fear, pleas, and hostility. We had about $150 and a few coins. Upon this revelation, the onset of disappointment and anger was apparent. We kept telling them that we did not have any more money but they refused to believe us. I could empathize with their anger and frustration. They came to rob us with high hopes, thinking we must have had good money to offer.

After a while, they sounded sort of "civil" with their acqui-
escence to the situation, saying we were not to blame after
all. The guy holding the gun was giving us the death stare
and probably shooting curses at us in his mind while iden-
tifying us with impossibly questionable bloodlines. It would
not have been too unwonted if he did. David wanted them out
of the house as soon as possible because he realized that the
longer they were in our home, the chances of something bad
happening became more likely. David kept it cool and played
it smart. He gave them his ATM card and PIN. The guy with
the gun threatened, "If the PIN doesn't work, we will return
to blow your heads off." I did not think he was serious about
blowing our heads off. I optimistically interpreted it as an
effective figure of speech. I bet that's something he says to
anyone with whom he had a financial transaction to complete.

They promptly made their way to the door, smashing
our vase along the way. They also pocketed our old stereo,
TV, and some coins on their way out. That was no big deal.
We collapsed down on the floor, against the wall, and sighed
in relief. As soon as I recovered from the shock, I reminded
David of the consequences of giving our visitors an incorrect
PIN. David assured me the PIN he provided was the correct
one. We were out of danger. We untied ourselves, gathered
our senses, and called the cops. David informed his bank
about the ATM card. Cops soon knocked on our door, jotted
down the event in their pads, and advised us to move out of

the neighborhood. Of course, we did not. We already knew the neighborhood was not exactly Henry Ford's neighborhood. We had no car at the time and we had to prioritize an efficient commute to the university. We had to stay close to the campus.

If my memory serves me right, David mentioned once that he bumped into one of those robbers in our neighborhood soon after the incident. It turned out that the guy was living two or three blocks from us. He informed David that he had been keeping tabs on David for some time. He had been keeping an eye on David's movements regularly after he observed David walking to the bus station in the mornings in his suit and tie, carrying a briefcase. It is worth mentioning that David was a good-looking man; couple that with a nice suit and tie and you have the perfect formula to pass as well-off. Naturally, once our visitor saw David in this fine ensemble, he thought David was loaded with green and decided on stalking him. I do not blame him for thinking David would be a good candidate to rob. So, he sought the aid of a professional with a gun. The problem was David had just gotten the job downtown and did not have enough time to accumulate cash. David mentioned that the robber had apologized for what happened that night. He also informed David that his partner kicked him out of the car once they left our home and did not give him his share. And we thought we were the ones who had had a bad night!

America has a complicated history with the painful legacy of slavery and the constant struggle to come to terms with race relations. There are deep, evident crevices of division among the people of this country between people who want to see the country as it is and people who want to see the country as it should be. The forces of the status quo are in constant conflict with the forces of change. These two opposing forces have been colliding with each other. History tells us that forces of change win in the end, sometimes at a high cost, as was the case in the Civil War. People can be very unyielding in their beliefs and, as a result, clashes are inevitable. Detroit kept reminding us of that from time to time.

Other than that, Detroit was fun. Nice campus, a small student body, and good friends.

I remember this old lady who used to live in one of the houses across from us. I cannot exactly recall what name she went by. We used to greet each other with "Hey, neighbor!" I remember her well because she was always this sweet woman who would wave at us, always smiling. People like her are probably handpicked and put on the face of Earth. We could always use more of them and their generous smiles. I reckon we are destined to meet a few of these nameless angels along the way as long as we are stopping and waving back! She lived alone. Her husband, who likely worked at the university, had passed away. She mentioned that she liked Detroit and enjoyed her own company here and thus she did not move out with her children. I met her often on my way to the campus. She would usually be watering her plants, cleaning the entryway to the door, and sometimes even cleaning the street in front of her house.

Once, I was scheduled for an interview. I was about to be late and decided to take my friend's car instead of advancing in my usual course, a five-minute walk to the bus stop before boarding the bus. Naturally, she saw me driving out and waved at me which I hadn't noticed. I was too preoccupied with the stress of getting to the interview on time. I drove away quite quickly. The interview went well (and yes, I managed to get there on the dot!). The next day, I was heading out for my usual 5-minute jaunt to the campus and I saw her. I waved and she beckoned me to come over for a chat. She inquired if I was alright, referring to my prior day's briskness. I could tell that she had been quite concerned about me since yesterday. I assured her that everything was alright and informed her of what had happened. She had never seen me driving before that day and that was the cause of her worry. After the chat, I walked away with a sense of warmth that reminded me of my mother's presence. Some "strangers" are just special that way. They might have just met you and yet care enough to notice the most minute details about you.

Detroit was a home away from home.

I have had a several jobs in the States, a few of them during my years at the university—campus jobs, and some afterward. It is not uncommon for an international student to work part-time on campus. I was one of the luckier ones because my family backed me up financially to cover some of my expenses, but one had to live quite the frugal man's life! Your Aunt Liza and your Uncle Karim helped me financially. I also got help from your Uncle Khaled.

When you are away from home, you experience a sudden sense of liberty that was otherwise alien to you in the past. You are on your own, and the world seems like your playground. I constantly met people who saw opportunities to test this newfound freedom. They, naturally, caved into temptation. America was this theme park and I suppose some might have felt that they had unbarred access to every ride (if they had cash to spare, of course). Freedom is never unbarred; there is always a price to pay. Most international students were responsible and disciplined. Back home freedom was not a prerogative: rather, one had to earn it. Money was something to be saved, cherished, and appreciated. Careless outlay of money was frowned upon, denounced even. So, you could imagine how a person might get dazzled when they find themselves under such liberal circumstances!

Time tested our customs and traditions handed down to us by our family, and we stood strong, mostly victorious.

We were told to rise early (encouraged to do the same during weekends too), to be respectful of money, and to be above succumbing to teenage means of entertainment or class bunking. You can already contemplate how unimagin-ably grave such an act was. I managed to discipline myself in order to nurture the freedom this land promised everyone. I guess I lucked out in this regard too because I was no stranger to freedom. Your grandfather had passed away young. Your grandmother was quite liberal. She trusted us to do the right things. We tried to do the same with both of you as well.

Complete autonomy without self-restraint can be dangerous, and some people had to learn that the hard way.

Hats were flung in the air, big smiles everywhere I looked, and just like that graduation day hastened beyond the horizon of time. I could only spectate. I got a degree in computer science. There wasn't much time to rejoice. The need for a well-paying job was now more crucial than ever. With degree in hand, I did not see any reason in going back to my part-time affairs. Thus, the search began and, sooner than I anticipated, came to a halt! I was not exactly over the top with hope but the picture was grimmer than I had expected. It was as if Lady Luck was unwaveringly working against me, FULL TIME! Help arrived at the eleventh hour when I had half-made my mind for returning to Bangladesh.

I had already moved to Arizona from Detroit by now. Your Aunt Liza had moved there from Iowa and I was crashing in with her.

My phone rang one morning as I lay in bed poring over the day's daily, my eyes scouring through the relevant pages one more time—a final shot at destiny before I packed up my things. It was a call from Ahmed, my cousin from Houston. He was working in a company over there. After the exchange of the usual pleasantries, I sulked about my dilemma. And then, as if the stars had decided to change their courses and side above and by me, Ahmed informed me of the news...

Ahmed invited me to come over to Houston to which I immediately agreed. I was on the edge of an emotional breakdown and I needed to unwind. "It can't get any worse than this," I thought to myself.

He was asking me to move there.

My curiosity peeked through the thick veil of despair, and I quizzed his insistence. He had an offer for me from his company. Everything fell into place like a charm; the obstacles that kept me worried for nights suddenly disappeared. The transition was quick and smooth, so smooth I do not remember how I felt when I was leaving Arizona behind. I was in Arizona for a short period of time. I joined his company writing software. Life changed like magic after that. My cousin greeted me with open arms. There is nothing like being with family.

One day I was working in my office in Houston and I received a call from a person. The voice from the other side belonged to a man who sounded in his mid-forties. My stay in the States taught me the hard way to throw curiosity out the window when you receive unexpected calls. Naturally, I was disgruntled, deeming the call as spam when the caller asked for me, but I humored him regardless with a couple of my minutes. I did not recognize him when he gave me his name but when he informed me that he was calling on behalf of a collection agency, the call did not seem unsolicited anymore. "Now that you have a job, how about paying up the money you owe to us?" The voice that sounded overtly nice moments ago was now a bit more assailed and businesslike.

He was talking about the student loan from the university. I had completely forgotten about the particular transaction but they did not. I was surprised he found me. I thought Texas was as far as I could get away from Detroit. Hmm, not far enough! (I am not, by any means of implication, suggesting that I was scheming to escape my debts, nor am I confessing to any felony!) Sometimes international students' office would give us a handwritten note to take to the registration office and they would let us register for the classes with the understanding that we would pay off the cost of the registration once our financial picture improved. My thoughts were cut short by his interruption when he said if I could put the entire amount of the money owed to the university on my credit card, then he would reduce the loan by twenty percent if I did so. He even knew I was carrying a credit card!

"It isn't like you are leaving me with many options," I rolled my eyes as I inwardly thought so to myself. I realized there was no escaping him. Fortunately, the loan was not a big amount although, money owed is never small or never easy to return! I gave him my credit card number.

After I hung up with him, I called David to find out if he had received a call from the collection agency. David acknowledged that he did. I felt a jab of regret when I learned that he had negotiated with them and got an even better deal than I did. It never occurred to me that I could have negotiated with the caller to reduce the burden of the loan further!

Ahmed and I used to commute to work together every day. We had a wonderful life in Houston. I was relieved because two were certainly better than one. Ahmed was great company and the Bengali community in Houston was very nice and supportive. Hospitality is innate in our culture.

Ahmed was two or probably three years younger than I. I do not know exactly. Sometimes you live around people for your whole life and you never get to know them, and then, as fate would have it, you move further and further away from each other only to reunite closer, stronger than ever. That was how I circled back with Ahmed. Back at home, we had not had the chance to hang out much, but Houston had other plans for us.

I found a friend and a brother who made my life in Houston easy. He helped me settle my affairs smoothly in Houston, and walked with me through the ordeal as I was beginning to understand the culture of the new company. I would have been on my own if it were not for him. He was always that way. Helping others came naturally to him. Sadly, as unpredictable and certain as it is, death drew Ahmed behind its dark curtains. He was quite young. Ahmed was one of the few finest human beings I knew. We miss him very much.

It is quite dispiriting...especially when one had to sit through one funeral after the other, watching many family members and friends join the choir invisible.

HOUSTON

The South has what I call tribal laws.

If you step onto someone's property by mistake you could get shot. If you fortuitously make someone's hackle rise, they could "jump on you with all four feet"! Detroit had seasoned me well with its display of misadventures and nuisances; I had survived Detroit with an important lesson: "Don't go looking for trouble when it's generally on the hunt 24/7." I was not going to let some itchy Texan ruin my life. I did not have the drive to challenge the ways here, and I did not go looking for that "drive." Why take the chance? So, I played it safe, staying within Houston city limits. I just got the job, I enjoyed working there, the pay was decent, and I had plans. I had a loan to repay, I needed to get my green card, and I needed to go home and see my family. "Not the best time to get shot!" I would say. I did not feel utterly out of place but I did feel that the demeanor of outsiders like myself was inapposite to that of the Texans and that not everyone exactly belonged to their clique.

However, things were easier since Houston was a cosmopolitan city. There were people from almost every corner of the globe. So, I was constantly around outsiders like myself. Apart from its unusual ways, Texas did not give me much to complain about. My Texan co-workers were very nice. Every spring I would drive along the highway to see the wildflowers and the wide-open country. That used to take the edge off from my nerves. Once I went to see a cave. I do not remember the name of the place but it was interesting exploring it. If the walls of that cave could talk, I bet they would have loved to tell me about all the visitors the cave had hosted before me. Not the plain, old, textbook history but the sort of history unrecorded, undoctored by human intervention, the sort of history that is anointed on the very walls of the cave. A presence that transcends eons which witnessed man and nature in contact can be sensed if you press your hand against the cool of the wall; you would not be the first to do so and you would not be the last.

I went to Bangladesh and tied the knot and your ammu came to Houston. I stayed for about four years in Houston and then moved to Missouri. Your ammu had gotten into a residency program at the University of Missouri medical school. I took a job at the university as a computer programmer.

MISSOURI

In the small town of Hannibal, Missouri,
when I was a boy, everybody was poor,
but didn't know it; and everybody was
comfortable and did know it.
— MARK TWAIN

Of all the places I lived in America, I was happiest living in Missouri.

When I was young two books made quite an impression on me. One was *Lost Horizon.* A faraway mystical place in the depths of the mountains of the Himalayas drew me with words that jumped out of the pages so I was able to visualize the imagery. It captivated my young mind so much that I started to foster a desire in my heart to go there one day. But that was then. The ever-punctual delivery personnel that is life, with one reality check after the next, kept knocking on my door, and over time Shangri-La was deposited away in the deepest cabinets of my mind. But it didn't fade away completely; I only shelved this private longing in the furthest drawers of my head and postponed it for someday in the future when I circle back to my memories, plans and...desires. From Marrakech to Rishikesh, from the ruins of the Parthenon to the alleys of Sidi Bou Said, and of course bathing under the sunset on the plains of the Serengeti, my desires to explore the exotic gifts of nature were being nurtured somewhere in the distance, away from the tug-of-war with life, only to find me when age and wisdom had finally managed to barter a certain degree of truce.

The other book was *The Adventures of Tom Sawyer.* I could easily picture myself in Tom's shoes with my time growing up in the village. Missouri was, or rather it still is, exactly the way I imagined it would be after reading *The Adventures of Tom Sawyer.* I could relate to his mischievous and intrepid nature and lifestyle. I was about fourteen years of age back in Bangladesh when I read *The Adventures of Tom Sawyer.* I think I found a copy of Twain's masterpiece in my father's library, the blue cover of a boy whitewashing fences caught my eye; the cover and the title appealed to my fourteen-year-old mind. The hardcover had a welcoming feel to it and I turned to the first chapter of Tom's adventures. I was immediately drawn to it.

Time has passed, the story of Tom Sawyer has been passed down through generations before and after me, and Twain today is still as relevant as he used to be. I remember how rapidly I flickered through the pages with ravenous anticipation and fixed absorption. I remember the lush green river and small pristine lakes. I remember strolling along the Mississippi in the 1840s in rolled-up jeans and shirt, and a straw hat. I was there with Tom... I was Tom!

From how I imagined Missouri would be to how it was when I explored it, Missouri did not disappoint; the adventure was (or is) always present in the air of Missouri. When your cousin Tazina came to visit us from London, we took her to Hannibal—Mark Twain's childhood home. We went inside the cave where Tom Sawyer got lost and lived through the fiction as if real.

There's so much that Missouri has given me. Aneesa was born in Columbia, Missouri. She brought so much joy into my life (you too, two years later. I have not forgotten you). With Aneesa, I found a toy to play with. With the addition of Aneesa and later you (in California) in my life, I had found a new purpose.

Looking back now, I left behind many fond memories in Missouri.

CALIFORNIA

After enjoying five beautiful, vibrant, yet short years in Missouri, we were beckoned to move again. Your ammu got a job in California and I also took a job as a programmer analyst. With its endless coastlines with picturesque towns, its deserts, forests, mountains and lakes, Universal Studios, Disneyland, Silicon Valley, and Hollywood (and the list goes on), the dainty and delicate state of California offered me much solace as a replacement for the Missouri we left behind.

California proved to be a rich repository of energy; there was a place for all sorts of people from every corner of the world in the Golden State. Everyone felt a sense of belonging in California: such was its air! Life was faster too, compared to what I was used to in Missouri. No wonder California is touted as the economic engine of the country.

As far as I am concerned California has two seasons: a mild, short winter, and summer. When it seems like the scorching breath of Death Valley extends to the entire state, one does get tired of sunshine every day; nobody is going to blame you for wishing for the occasional rain in summer. I am also guilty of the sentiment; a little rain now and then does not sound too bad but I do not have complaints most of the time.

I guess you could say that I have been seasoned by two contrasting climates in my lifetime. On one hand, you have the climate of California—there is practically no changing of seasons other than mild winter and warm summer—and on the other there is Bangladesh where there are six seasons! The year is a magnificent assortment of colors. Nature blesses the West and East differently, I suppose. For instance, Autumn in America showers the streets with leaves of yellow and brown and brushes you with nature through its earth.

Autumn in Bangladesh, contrarily, sketches the sky with a different color every quarter of the day and blesses you by nature from above. Mother Nature personally takes matters into her hands to paint each of her aspects with a different color every season. And the colors are just visually unignorable. Mother Nature is so fond of Bangladesh that she graces the country with another autumn after the first – Late Autumn. It is all just so wonderful, especially if you live in the countryside; one can fully experience nature in all its glory! The bonds that a Bangladeshi countryman shares with nature are one—that of an artist and the canvas. If you think that it is the man who dwells the brush, you are in for a treat! Nature colors according to its wishes. Seasons are reminders that man and nature are very much attuned to each other. We influence each other in our grand and humble ways; when one lives or grows up in the countryside, they begin to realize it before others.

The changes in the country are just so vivid. The air starts to smell different. The sky dresses itself up in a different hue every season, sometimes a couple of times at least to mark the time of the day! A new season demands the assembly of new food. The imminent new harvest of winter signals that changes in the breakfast menu were in order, and soon enough dome-shaped rice cakes, as white as half-snowballs, sometimes stuffed with carefully portioned molasses and coconut flakes, would be stacked on the breakfast table along with milk that has been simmered until it is thickened with it owns aroma. Now, you dip the rice cakes in the milk or you could indulge yourself with some more jaggery: help yourself to as much as you want. Women in the village, with seemingly effortless expertise, would make them and deliver them at home early in the morning.

And hence, every season in Bangladesh inspires poets and songwriters to further their craft... Countless poetry and songs are written for every season.

MEMORIES

We grow up learning that nothing lasts forever; we grow up learning that life is all about a series of ups and downs, that good times follow the bad, and that cycle continues until the end of our times. What makes me wonder is how we are never able to accept this cycle. We hope for something good to happen sometime soon, or we anticipate that something bad is going to happen anytime now. We do so when we realize (or like to think) that this moment is the epitome of our leading emotions, happy or sad, and this moment is the point where things could go uphill or down. We can guess that things are going to turn for the better or worse and yet it catches us off-guard. Whether it is a draft of bad luck or a miraculous fortune, we anticipate it and yet never see it coming. I reckon that it is unpredictable nature that slips through our unwary spot. The truly lucky ones catch the "good-times-train" and continue to land on a happy station .

Hence, unwatchful, inattentive, and in a fool's paradise, I too was unwary.

After a few years in California, life started to unravel. Everything started to fall apart. The universe which was so generous to me only yesterday came after me with full fury. I could see the dark cloud looming on the horizon. I remember the night when I moved out of the house.

It was past your bedtime, and I knew you and Aneesa were asleep. I walked over to your room and went in with slow, soft steps; softly because I wanted to avoid the risk of waking you up, and slowly because I was not ready for this moment to end. The sight of you two tucked under your blankets, peacefully dreaming, was not one I wanted to let go of. The calm expressions that you two wore in your sleep were enough to calm the raging storm in me… momentarily. With a deep sigh, I walked over to you, one by one, and caressed you both.

I turned for my exit. I was bleeding inside. I did not dare look back. I had to summon all my strength to fight that temptation of looking back for another glimpse because I knew if I did, all my resolve would melt into nothingness; things had gone too far for me to turn back. As soon as I walked out of your room, I found my speed and paced out of the front door.

I came to my apartment and walked up the stairs. Those were the longest stairs I ever had to climb. My legs felt like lead against the cold surface of the stairs, and I had to drag them up inch by inch. There was no tune of triumph when I made it into my room. The silence was only temporarily pierced when I crashed my weight on the bed; then it… silence… reigned again.

Every evening I came to an empty apartment like a wounded soldier, defeated in a battle who went back out in the world because that was the bare minimum he ought to do for protecting his existence. Life constantly felt like a series of obstacles. I was piling up one failure after the other; as soon as I climbed over one mountain, I found myself standing right in front of another one that challenged my determination which at this point felt like a burden. I wanted to give up so badly. I felt like fighting a formidable enemy, and this enemy was not going to let me win.

Soon the expected ensued; depression came to my company. The worst part of the day was early morning when a cloud of despondency would paralyze me in bed, and I would force myself out of the blanket, and then face a world that I had no intention of facing.

It was like pushing a cart with no wheels on it. I had become heavy for myself. Even paying a simple bill would become an insurmountable task. The heart was in one place and the mind aloof! No amount of medication could have soothed my depression, let alone make it go away. Dealing with depression had become a task within itself. My remedy was elsewhere; if I had them, I was fit and fine. When Aneesa and you were with me, my depression was gone. Only joy followed.

Your and Aneesa's absences naturally fashioned the necessity for alternatives; a man on the brink of complete loss had to forage to make do. The will to keep surviving is inbred into the very cells of man: as long as there is a soul, he must keep living... or surviving... even at that state of loss, even if it means surviving in a state of meaningless existence. And so, I found myself foraging even more deeply into our memories, salvaging and re-watching through the reels that play on the display which pops up when you close your eyes... I just could not wait to get home, turn out all the lights and play the "good times" every day...

Sometimes I would drop by your school before the bell. While waiting for you outside, I would wonder how your day had been. I would wonder if you would have something interesting to share with me while we waited for the bell to ring.

The cacophony of bustling children sprinting out the entrance and pouring on to the soft grass was indeed a sight that I enjoyed. The school grounds would be filled with kids of all sizes. And I would get busy trying to spot my genes amidst the crowd. "There you are!" As soon as you saw me, you would run towards me and kiss me.

Remember when you used to take me to your classroom on the days when I would come to see you at school? I would help you set up the chairs in the room. Chairs would always be stacked on top of the desk if I remember correctly.

When you moved to the upper classes, I noticed it immediately. There was a change in routine. You did not kiss me when you saw me in your school anymore, especially in front of your friends. You became a little self-conscious...

That is part of growing up.

Your kindergarten teacher had one issue with you, that you used to daydream in the class; no sugarcoating, plain and dry. She might not have been wrong, and I think I know what the problem is. And you may have gotten it from me. I used to do the same back in elementary school. There you go, the secret is out! I wonder what went on in that head of yours. I still do. Did you and I, two "great minds," "think alike"?

I used to call Aneesa. Did you know? When I wanted to know what was going on with you, I would call Aneesa because you would tell me nothing. And she had your back... always! Never snitched on you, not once! And she also handled the conversation with blunt diplomacy. The way she put it was that there was conscious action of disengagement in certain situations because if you had carelessly let an answer slip to one of my questions, then you ran the risk of encountering a follow-up question from me which would require another answer from you, and that might have, in turn, developed into a conversation—something you find utterly distasteful. So says Aneesa, the wise one.

Has a father ever won with his children in the history of fatherhood? I doubt it. My dear Aneesa had an entirely different effect on me and the effect lingers on even in nostalgia...

When Aneesa was two years old and I would leave her at the daycare center, she would press her face on the glass door with the saddest expression that I have ever seen! She would keep staring at me until I was out of her sight. Once I was out of her view, she would turn away from the door and find herself a place to sit facing away from the door. I would check on her from a distance, out of her sight, and Aneesa's despair at the door to me was a symbol of her despair to me! It was as if she had thought I had temporarily disowned her and given her away to the daycare. The sight of my little girl supposedly giving up on me would prove to be too much for my guilty conscience; I could not stand in the shadows and keep up my act of being strong. And then, I would immediately go in and pick her up.

After bringing her home I would turn the VCR on, and she would lie on a sofa and watch "Cinderella" without blinking her eyes, every day. The Cinderella on the screen was of little interest to me, I knew everything about her. The Cinderella who lay on the couch had my undivided attention, I wanted to learn everything about her.

I do not remember Aneesa ever crying when she was a baby. We could rely on her to be alone on her own. We would put her in the crib and leave. She would keep herself busy with her usual affairs and when she got tired from all the hard work, she would fall asleep on her own; and she would never wake up in the middle of the night and cry (unlike some other guy I knew of!).

She was not fussy about many things, food especially. We could just leave the food in front of her and watch her eat with Zen-like concentration. We could tell that she enjoyed her time with the tasks she had. She would eat macaroni and cheese every day and then one day I would notice that she would not finish her portion of macaroni and cheese. I would swap the mac and cheese with fried chicken. Everything would again be back to normal, her plates would come back squeaky clean, her way of informing us that she had moved on to fried chicken now. I would buy her fried chicken every day. After a while, she would go for something else and never mention fried chicken again. Aneesa was what I call "Toyota Kid." Trouble-free! You, on the other hand, would declare war on food. You did not like rice which was strange given your Asian origin. But you used to love broccoli, which was another strange thing about you. Never, before you came into my life, had I met a kid who loved broccoli so much. You could have been a poster child for the broccoli growers!

You both were two different sides of the same coin; at least that was the case when it came to how you looked at things. Was it challenging for us? Yes. Was it fun? Definitely!

Grades, yes, there was the pressing and burning issue of grades. Aneesa would come home and would triumphantly declare that she got an "A"- that was always the context. And it was always an uneventful moment for her, we never ceased to be surprised and proud. But with you, it was a challenge and I still never ceased to be surprised. When I asked you about your grades, you would say your grades were in the mail. I asked you again a week later and your answer was still the same: your grades were coming in the mail. So, I did what any other father would have done in the same situation, I just gave up after a while. What's the point? Needless to say, the problem was not with the postal service! But since you got admitted to an excellent school, I assumed your grades were good. One had to console oneself in one way or the other!

My nights in California were not always filled with embracing nostalgia. Some nights were interrupted by occurrences that pushed their way into my memory book without my control. I woke up in the middle of one night to a commotion.

As I lay in bed, unenthusiastic about the idea of getting up (which had become a norm by then), I could hear people talking and pacing around my house. It was the type of scurrying that suggested something serious. I was at a crossroads: "I don't want to be a part of this, but this seems like an emergency!" Much to the disinterest of one part of me, I got up and opened the door to check what was happening. The night was lit with blue and red lights, and I could make out a few of the outlines of navy blue against the two colors; the cops had already intervened.

An officer stepped towards me and informed me that they had apprehended a man. I peeked over the officer to see a young man sitting on the curb in front of my home. I could only see his handcuffed back. Regardless of his back turned to me, I could make out that he was defeated and tired.

I returned to bed. The commotion died down sooner than I had anticipated. In the renewed silence of the night, I thought about this young man; his defeated and exhausted silhouette in the blue and red-lit night kept coming back to me when I shut my lids, and I felt sad. When he was a child, he must have been a joy to his mother and his mother must have had dreams for him. She must have dreamed and wished that one day her son would grow up to be a fine young man, make society a better place, and she would be proud of him. What would his mother be feeling tonight upon receiving the news? Devastated? I am sure. Today he is the cause of a mother's anguish.

But he was young; there was still time. He could still turn his life around, and I wished he did.

HOME

It is a question rather out of the blue but can you climb a tree? What is the tallest tree that you ever climbed on? Do you immediately think of climbing one as soon as you see a tall tree? I think there is something primitive, at least till that certain age of life, about our sudden urges to mount the tallest tree. Could it be our drive to brave the tallest, biggest "monument" that would qualify us to take on the next taller, bigger monument? Or could it be the lofty evolutionary trait of trying to reach the above and the beyond which eventually prompted us to stand upright? Either way, I would like to conclude that a longing to climb trees entreats the minds of every man and woman alike, at least once in our lives.

The triggers for nostalgia or pining are rather strange: you could be comparing your past and the present, diagnose what the present is missing and be nostalgic, or you could find the existence of similar pieces in both frames of time and still be nostalgic. Or, on a fine summer day, you could just be doing nothing and the soothing breeze of the past could catch you off-guard with a gentle caress on the shoulder; the mind works in mysterious ways!

I suppose one reaches a certain point in life where their subconscious becomes very welcoming to the pleasant visits of unexpected nostalgia; my mind has been acting the same for some time. I must admit, I do enjoy these flashbacks.

My mind surfs through the oceans, and speeds through thousands of miles to a little village in Bangladesh. It knows exactly what its destination is. It knows where to stop. When my mind realizes that we are close, it does not slow down and relish the rest of the road; no, it speeds up, overworking the lungs and muscles, without halting even while flinging the gates open, until it finally stops at the very last step only to stop from crashing with the door, that brown slab of wood with designs that have collected dust and collected memories, the very familiar brown door that marks the entrance to your grandparents' home. My heart, giddy with childlike impatience, cannot wait to open it. My mind, withholding for reasons unknown and finally tired of acting mature, concurs. With both hands extended, the door is opened carefully as if something unexpected would grapple me from the inside. Instead, I feel a warm embrace of memories; some that I did not realize existed until that moment.

My childhood was so different from the way you grew up here in America. I grew up with my siblings and my parents. Days that were considered ordinary then strike as celebrations now that I think about them. We spent a good part of the day climbing on trees and plucking fruits, fishing, and playing with our nephews and friends.

The various seasons of Bangladesh would yield jewels on the tree. They came in different hues, sizes, shapes, and tastes. I and the contemporaries of my age would take it upon ourselves to monitor the neighborhood fruit-bearing trees and do inventory. We would check on these "jewels" on our way to school and on our way back home. When the time and fruits were ripe, with much gusto, hours of scheming would ensue every week until the moment of plucking had come. Depending on the season, it could be guava, mango, plum, berries, jackfruits, lychees, and many other fruits. I do not even know what some of them are called in English.

There was a thrill in climbing on the tallest branch of a tree and snatching guava before one of my friends could have gotten it first. Have you ever tasted jackfruit? I reckon not. It is a big fruit.

How do you tell if jackfruit is ripe? You tap the fruit with your finger on different spots and listen for the right sound.

How did I come by this knowledge? Years of experience! The right sound would signal that the fruit was ready to be devoured. When we could finally hear it, our restive faces would be overcome with wild excitement. With skill no less than that of a surgeon we would split the fruit in the middle and flatten it. Four of us would sit around the fruit and feast on it! We were required to get our hands dirty, literally and figuratively.

The neighborhood trees were not the only ones that we stormed. We had an orchard. My uncle collected plants, mostly fruit trees from all over India, and planted them in the orchard. There were a few rare fruit plants that I have not seen anywhere. This was our hangout spot and we used to spend a lot of our gleeful hours in this orchard. There were always some fruits we could pick. I wanted to show you this orchard, so you could have seen *Abbu*'s hangout place.

Lychees... that fruit brings back an interesting memory.

During one regular summer afternoon, when everyone else was dozing off from their afternoon meal and we were up to no good (as usual), we decided to have our way with the lychee tree in the orchard. Our usual band was plotting out the next shenanigans when one of us noticed the water buffalo with unusually long horns. When we approached it, we realized that the caution that we weathered to get close to it was unneeded for the dark-shaded animal had no intention of provoking the group of four-foot-tall midgets that advanced towards it; it was too busy munching on the patch of grass under the lychee branch to throw care at us. It cast a glance at the four boys that were not there a while ago and went back to grinding the grass between its upper jaw against the lower with not a care in the world! When our initial sentiment about the buffalo faded away, curiosity set in, and like men always do when they are with friends and too comfortable, we tried to make the situation more "interesting" by adding the element of thrill to it. Seeing that the buffalo did not pose the risk of charging at us, one of us dared the rest to mount on top of it.

That was the dare that ought to satisfy the frivolous greed for our entertainment! And so—call it the need to prove his courage to his peers or something else—we all volunteered with much fervor! After a much-needed encouragement from my gang members, I decided to ride the buffalo first. We cautioned closer and patted it; not bothered still. I got on top of the buffalo carefully heeding to not irritate the animal with help from my friends. I stared at the beings below me and felt a rush of adrenaline; I was ready to do anything! I focused on the performance which I was about to execute. Begging my nerves to retain vigilance, I transferred both my feet on the back of the buffalo for balance in case the animal decided it had too much of us.

It did not move.

My confidence elevated twofold, I displaced myself completely on its back and anchored a firm grip with my toes. The warm, smooth skin of the buffalo felt like a blanket that wanted to slip under my feet. I sat comfortably and ready to ride the buffalo, and the others, now marveling at what I had managed to do, beckoned me to complete the final task and pave the way for their turn. The bunch of lychees overhead stared at me from a distance above, like a spearhead waiting to descend on me. Someone slapped the rear side of the animal and for obvious reasons, the buffalo did not like it and started to run. The branch of the lychee tree hit me on my chest. Before I knew what had happened the "ground" under me slipped past me, and I slumped onto the hard surface.

In a feeble attempt to block the unpleasant experience that was to set its course through me, I probably had closed my eyes. I opened them when I heard my peers talking rather frantically. I was on the ground and my friends circled me.

I had survived the crash but the hand which extended itself to survive the fall did not! I fractured my left hand. I stood up and saw my arm dangling from my shoulder. The pain didn't set in until they had pointed toward my hand. And like an uninvited guest, pain pierced through my muscles and bone. I could feel different degrees of pain in different regions of my body. My back screamed from the hard landing on the ground. We rushed home, the left hand dangled abnormally. As confident as we felt about facing everything in our path head-on, the miracles of medicine were one lesson we had not mastered yet!

I went to a nearby town and the doctor put a plaster on my hand. After one month when the plaster was removed, I could not straighten my hand. Another problem. My mother called a village medicine man. He held my arm and gave it a sudden jerk!

Crack! I suppose the bone had finally found its location. It hurt but was tolerable. He came for a few days and massaged my arm with an ointment that he made, and after a few days my hand was as good as new.

We had a large field patched with grass in front of our home. We used to play there. This open space is gone now. The land is being used for agriculture. One day we were playing and heard someone weeping. A covered bull cart was passing by, like the ones we see in western movies only pulled by two oxen. Inside that wagon, a young girl was weeping. Her sobs were audible enough for us to stop our activity and gather at the boundary of the field. We were not unacquainted with such a scene and yet every time we came across one, we had to stop in our tracks. It didn't quite rub well with our morals if we continued our activities when someone about our age was crying.

She was leaving her father's love and care and was off to a hostile territory—her in-laws' home. Unlike us, her playful days had suddenly ended, and she would soon be dealing with life's harsh realities. For a teenage girl who was practically a child, that is a frightening experience. From her expression and the looks akin to countless before and after her, I doubted that the environment in the new territory was going to be as loving and caring as her father's. Maybe my doubts and her fears came from the same place; no wonder she was weeping on her way to this new domain because she had no choice, and we could only stand and pray the best for her because we had no choice.

There is just a myriad of memories in that orchard. Half of my childhood was consumed with running and playing in it. But some years back when I went to my village, I could not find our orchard. I was shocked. The government had built a long and wide irrigation canal right through the orchard. Not a single tree stands today. I do not think it would be an overstatement to say that my fertile village which nourished and nurtured us once, stands deserted today; so much has changed. It is not the same without the people who made the barren piece of land cozy; some we have lost to the insurmountable space which is a no-mortal territory while others we have lost to the distance of the unknown. Such a tragedy!

Our village would host an unusual visitor from time to time. A concierge, a young Mahout would guide our visitor from village to village, house to house. And at every door the elephant would approach, people would give it food.

It is common knowledge that these huge mammals need to consume a considerable amount of food to "stay in shape." There were forests in these extensive human habitats to provide for this domesticated animal. Displaying the majestic animal around the village was the only way for the owner of the elephant to keep his maintenance costs down.

My nephews and I are of the same age, and when kindred youths of the same age gather, they usually cook up the perfect recipe for some black-hearted delinquency. We were no different back in the day! One day, when we were in the fifth grade, we decided to smoke cigarettes. I do not recall who brought it up but we all agreed in perfect sync to go along with his wishes to "look cool." Without much deliberation, the four of us pitched in our pocket money and bought a cheap pack of cigarettes. The pack was handed over to the most "responsible" of the bunch for safekeeping; we could count on him to conjure up some trick to save the whole lot if we were caught by any eyes of suspicion. The pack of cigarettes cautiously tucked in the vest beneath his shirt and with the rest of us flocking around him like unnerved bodyguards, we headed for our orchard. No place like home to cook Satan's meal!

While we tried to act as what might have been thought normal at that time, it might have as well been our most out-of-place performance put together. We paced briskly, barely met eyes, and kept our interactions with villagers we met to a minimum. Everyone seemed to be on to us (or so it seemed!). As they say, a guilty conscience is always suspicious. Finally, we arrived at the orchard. We selected the tree that bears witness to our legends—the lychee tree in our orchard! We climbed on its highest branch, and looked around to ensure that the coast was clear; each choosing a spot to their comfort and to camouflage themselves under the canopy of the tree. We all looked at our "carrier" and signaled him to take out the "package." The other three landed a helping hand with whisking the packet out; four white and brown sticks were dealt out to each member like cards. Like white cranes, we stretched our necks in four directions and the whole ritual of ensuring it was safe for us was performed again. Once the first one had mustered all the courage to light his cigarette, it was easy for the rest to follow. We tried to keep the coughing down lest someone was to hear us. We had our shirts unbuttoned to the last three, and every time we succumbed to coughing, we would dig our heads inside the crevice of our shirts to muffle the noise. We saw a man walking towards our home. We were sure he did not see us but he did. He saw that thin white cloud of smoke conjured by the four boys around the lychee tree. He had informed the matter at home. We washed our mouths, chewed a few mint leaves each, and returned home thinking everything was under control. And could we have been more wrong? My elder brother called me, put his hand inside my pocket, and found the packet with a few leftover cigarettes. Yes, the cat's out of the bag—I was the carrier!

I received one slap. My nephew Taufiq, my sister's son, was visiting us, so he escaped without a scratch. And then Mithu, my other nephew, received most of the brunt of the attack from one of his cousins, the son of my first cousin. My other nephew Rubel, the remaining culprit, ran out of home as soon as he saw the treatment I and Mithu had received. When he returned home, I am unsure of. We washed, had a meal, went outside, and played soccer. Sometimes we played soccer with a grapefruit. Grapefruits in Bangladesh are quite big; you just yank one from the tree and start the game. They never last long though; after a few goals, you had to yank a new one down. And after a few goals, we all had forgotten the whole incident.

Some things, however, are not forgettable, an incurable loss, for instance. Sadly, Rubel had passed away.

Ironically, Mithu, among the four of us, developed a liking for cigarettes in the later years. Yes, Mithu, the very one who was treated most harshly by his cousin; you would think he had learned his lesson and would be the one to stay away from cigarettes but he did not. Once I asked him how he became a smoker since he was the one who took most of the brunt of the attack.

"Maybe my brother didn't beat me hard enough," he replied with his usual playful humor.

Mithu studied economics and found a job in the same field but later quit it, got involved in business, and became a successful businessman. Mithu has always been the first one to call me every time I visited Bangladesh; he would ask me and some of our family for dinner at a restaurant. He has been doing this for the last three decades! I have been back to Bangladesh numerous times over the years, and he made it a point to get the old group together every time I was there. Mithu would call us and tell us which restaurant to come over to, and we would go. He would arrive with a big grin and he would take care of the rest. It would be a celebration of life and this always became the venue for all of us catching up, and the venue for me receiving additional invitations to dinner from the rest, but it would always be Mithu to invite everyone first. I think he looked forward to these occasions and contested his previous efforts to arrange for the whole event before anyone else! How many nephews do you know who would do this?

Most people are just about the same but occasionally you come across individuals who would stand out; they will leave their mark and you grow a longing to be around them or see more of them. When Mithu entered a room, the room would come to life automatically. He just carried that aura that would uplift the morale of the people around him. Mithu was a generous, warm soul; people around him knew that. Mithu was their go-to guy if they ever needed help with something. He tried to always be there for everyone, always helping people out of financial predicaments the best he could.

When I was in Bangladesh in 2020, I stayed with him. That was the last time I saw him. It was such an enjoyable stay—a sleepover just like old times; we reminisced about our childhood years. He took me to all these different places that opened while I was away in the States, and as always, he paid the bill!

I inform you this with a heavy heart, Mithu passed away in 2021. The news was hard on all of us. Mithu thrived in chaos, noise, and among people—"the more the merrier"—he lived by that motto. A quiet life was not for him. If you enter heaven and you hear someone talking and shouting while everyone else around is laughing, that's Mithu.

He will be missed.

I, like most other adults, am aware that a certain essence of life is loss, and you would think after learning an important lesson as such, we would come to terms with this equation of life: you live, you love, and you die. This is one lesson that is, although learned, never easily accepted. Humans are programmed to take their losses personally; they spend their lives trying to make up for one loss and then stumble across the next. My losses are too unbearable to count. I have already lost all five brothers, three sisters, sisters-in-law, brothers-in-law, nephews, many family members, and friends. You get used to having people around you; their absences are missing pieces of a puzzle—without them, the picture is incomplete. Yes, time does make us forget that they once laughed with us and breathed the same air that we did but time, quite heartlessly, again reminds us of them. And with the last person gone, that picture fades away.

I can see my picture fading; those whose love and affection I grew up with are leaving. Those who used to bring me joy and laughter are gone. Too many deaths around me, it is overwhelming. Loss is probably one of the languages life uses to communicate with us; loss is life's way of reminding us, again and again, to not take our loved ones for granted.

Life is a teacher, sometimes an unforgiving teacher – the type that rarely acquiesces in giving us a second chance to make things right.

TEACHERS

Speaking of teachers, have I ever told you how I was introduced to schooling for the first time? It happened when I was about five years old; one fine day I was playing in the front yard of our elementary school in the village. A teacher (long-sleeved shirts with *lungi* or trousers and a black umbrella- one could tell a schoolteacher apart from the rest in those days because they had a deliberately dressed stereotype to stand out among others!) approached me. Curious enough, I stopped playing and he asked me if I wanted to come to school. I foolishly replied "yes"- seemed like a good idea at the time. Sigh! A tragic mistake!

He asked me to go home and bring some money- the fees required to get enrolled. The amount he quoted was probably worth a quarter at the time. I went home and told my father about it. My father was probably surprised but being the man of few words that he was, he did not ask any questions. Instead, he reached into his pockets and tossed a coin at me. I grabbed the coin, returned to the school, found the teacher, and handed over the change to him. He tossed the change into his pocket (that is his cigarette money) and said,

"Come to school tomorrow. You are in grade one."

And I was in.

Now, compare that to the admission to your school. Not only did we fill out a bunch of forms, but we had to provide the school with your immunization records!

The math teacher in my school was super strict. He used to carry a bamboo stick. We feared him more than the imaginary ghosts under our beds! He was such a high threat level that we used his name to issue the ultimate warning if any of our peers tried to act smart. The mathematics sir was the harbinger of justice and fear!

In second grade he would queue us up and quiz the multiplication tables. Sometimes we were required to recite the complete table of a number, and, if luck was grim for someone, they would be interrogated and grilled with arbitrary multiplication expressions from all the tables in the term. We were allowed only a second to reply. Had we not in military tenor shouted out the answer in a second, we were expected to extend our hand forward without delay. With terror-stricken eyes, some would watch the bamboo stick lifted to an unpleasant height while others would rather look away or close their eyes shut and brace for impact! The stick would descend swiftly on the palm of our hands once. Ouch!! That is how we learned multiplication tables, just so you know. If you find that shocking, you would be stunned to know that we did not dislike this teacher. We respected all our teachers. You should know teachers are revered in eastern cultures.

We did not know his name. He was known by the place he hailed from. We called him "Khutamara sir." He was from a village named Khutamara. A few years back I went to my hometown and asked six people if they knew his actual name; I got six different names. I tried, but maybe he never cared much for recognition by his name, or the fact that no one knew his name was unknown to him. His reputation had surpassed such trivial forms of identification. I suppose he was content with his title: "sir" and his responsibility to teach. His mission was to teach, and he did. Then there was Mr. Aminur or "Aminur sir." He was another of my elementary school teachers. Mr. Aminur was free-spirited, enthusiastic, and optimistic. In his younger years, he used to go hunting, mostly for birds. One day the shell of the gun got stuck inside his gun. He took a long stick and tried to dislodge the shell. The gun went off, sending two of his fingers flying in the air. That was the end of his plans for any future hunting expeditions.

It was during the fifth grade that we came to know of the district-wide test that fifth graders took to prove their mettle. This was a test eyed by students, teachers, and parents equally because, if you had passed this test, you would be awarded a government scholarship (money); additionally, if you managed to get the scholarship, you would become an instant "star" at that age and be revered as a top tier student in the community. My nephew Mithu and I decided to take this test. Since this was our first time, we needed to be guided. Aminur was the one you sought to study. He was the coach. He took great pride if any of his students passed this test. When he heard of our plans of taking the test, he immediately enrolled us as his protégés. Thus, under his mentorship, our apprenticeship commenced. We would go to his home and study diligently. Aminur wielded a trade secret—he had a very old and thick arithmetic book.

There was also a table, burnished to replicate oak brown, sometimes accompanied by a slip of a drawer coupled with a flimsy lock—a very simple article of furniture that almost every household of the time possessed. Simple as it was, the addition of it in the household was not merely for decoration; no, it was a symbol of a household that considered education a rather serious business. It was on these wooden apparatuses that most studying took place, these oak brown tables or makeshift short desks under which you could tuck your lower half as you prepared to undertake your academic labors. They also doubled down as sitting furniture! The interior of the house lit up in the orange shade from the oil lamps; rhythmic recitation of lessons filled the dark silence. All individual readings, if one listened closely, created a chorus of kids dealing with their lessons; half of them fearing Khutamara sir's dancing stick and the rest aspiring for scholarships.

Aminur had similar arrangements in his household for his students. Chairs would be drawn for our accommodation around the table and we would surround him on two corners of his table. Our stationery and notebooks would be unloaded on our side of the table while Aminur placed the Arithmetic book and the oil lamp in between. Once the said circumstances were laid out, we would commence solving problems from this book.

On the day of the test, he walked with us to the test center which was about one and a half-mile from our home; he knew what our strengths and weaknesses were and like the fine teacher he was, boosting our morale and keeping us grounded, he offered us advice and suggestions on the way. "Save the troublesome problems for later; don't dwell too much on them." "Stay calm and focused." "Don't forget to skim through the formulas one last time before the test." Then, after walking us as far into the premises as guardians were allowed, he anxiously waited for us the whole time. At the end of the test, we all walked back home.

When we passed this exam, my mother invited all the teachers from our school to lunch. She cooked a wonderful meal for them.

After retiring from school, Aminur started practicing homeopathic medicine which is not too uncommon in that part of the world, especially in Bengal. One would get hold of a homeopathic medicine book and start practicing medicine. Some practice this branch of medicine as a hobby.

When I was living in Bangladesh, I could have visited my schoolteachers anytime I wanted. I had access but that thought never crossed my mind. Now, I want to see them but they are gone. It is like I arrived at the station but the train had already left. I was late.

ROOTS

As a prerogative of being born in a Bangladeshi household, a certain segment of history has always been part of your upbringing. I am aware that contemporary parents of my generation often talk quite fondly of this part of history because we are sort of entitled to talk about it! Therefore, let me use this opportunity to add a historical event of India to your repertoire of the past—when the British first set foot in Bengal, India, in the eighteenth century.

Their arrival had already upset Mughal India's control over the land, and their presence caused tumultuous fracases which spread across India. Bengal, too, got involved and the skirmishes of the Brits with the then-Nawab of Bengal, Siraj-ud-Daulah, soon took the shape of a full-out war. Things were looking good for Bengal's Nawab but took a bleak turn when Siraj-ud-Daulah's Commanding General, Mir Jafar, cut a deal with the British. When the two armies met face to face at the plain of Plassey, Mir Jafar did not engage his army and the Nawab was defeated in 1757. It was an important victory for the British. It paved the path toward the eventual

British Raj in India. Ever since, Mir Jafar's betrayal earned his name a special degree of infamy in Bengal. After the war, his name stomached the mark of stigma (rightfully so!) which soon evolved into the worst title for anyone who engaged in treachery. During elections, during the usual name-calling sessions in campaigns, a politician would call his opponent Mir Jafar now and then. That is the worst name you could call a Bengali. Poor Mir Jafar, he probably did not realize the extent of his actions at the time.

One of Nawab's soldiers later settled in the northern part of Bengal, in Rangpur. My grandfather, Munir Uddin Chowdhury, was the descendant of this soldier so I was told.

Nawab Siraj-ud-Daulah became a folk hero in Bangladesh and West Bengal, India. His story is popular in the moviemaking and playwriting community. Schools host annual events and have children play dramas on him (and one of those unlucky kids probably gets picked for the role of Mir Jafar!). I too once played a part in Siraj-Ud-Daulah's story when I was in third or fourth grade, still living in our village. Your grandfather was alive at the time. One of the usual suspects, Mithu, my cousin-brother's son, wanted to play the leading role, Siraj-ud-Daulah. We were of the same age. Naturally, we both wanted to play the hero. In the end, I decided to be the bigger person and let him take the role.

I played Robert Clive, the British military officer. Your grandfather had an English hat that he used to wear when he would go hunting in the jungles of India during the British Raj. I wore that hat in the play. Mithu too dressed appropriately for his role. At the end of the play, there was a scene where Mithu and I were to start fighting with our tin swords. Mithu was scheduled to drop dead after five minutes of fighting but he would not; he kept fighting with me, he got too invested in his role, I guess! When the cue was missed, everyone realized that Mithu was just too imbued in his role, and it was at this moment it occurred to us that we had a situation on our hands. The audience was shouting at Mithu, telling him to drop his sword and hit the floor, but he refused. He just would not come to terms with the fact that in this case the hero of the story lost the war and had to die. Man becomes immortal by dying, not by living, but who was going to tell him that in the middle of our "war"? His idea of heroes was that heroes always win; sadly, for him, this hero did not. Had he been informed in advance that Siraj-ud-Daulah lost the war and was killed, he probably would not have tried so hard to get the role in the first place!

History must be told as it was. Mithu could not have possibly been expecting me to go down and believe that his victory would somehow rewrite the course of history! He was determined to win this fight and was fighting hard. We were both panting, both unwilling to meet our theatric demise. With dents all over their lengths, our swords had started to break apart. What was to happen now?

Olympian gods lost their cool and decided to intervene.

Someone jumped on stage and whacked Mithu down to the floor. The play ended. The applause broke in. History was preserved.

Some histories do not make it to the threshold of academia or even do not end up in the footnotes of history books and yet they survive; this genre of history survives through word of mouth, handed down through generations. Munir-uddin Chowdhury, my grandfather, "his-story" stuck around in time in a similar fashion.

My grandfather was a fanatical buyer of land. As soon as he had saved some money, he would buy land. We do not have photos of him but I was told he was short, an average guy. And soon he became the owner of large areas of land, just like his father!

Lord Cornwallis was the Governor-General of Bengal in the eighteenth century. He was in America during the American Revolutionary War before he was assigned to India. In 1793, he introduced a system of collecting taxes from farmers/landowners. People had to buy the right to collect taxes in an auction. My grandfather bought this right with large sacks of money (There were no checks in those days! I am not exactly sure what kind of currency they used in those days.), which granted him the right to collect taxes from a large swath of land consisting of many villages. Even after paying royalties to the British, he was hauling in a huge sum of money. Later he added more areas to his coffer. This system of collecting taxes was called Permanent Settlement, which meant he and his children would continue to collect taxes. Great deal! Good times rolled in. But as all good times must come to an end, this system of collecting taxes was abolished when India got independence and Pakistan was created long before I was born. So, I have not seen my family's golden days, only heard stories about it.

When my grandfather was alive, long before I was born, our house burned down twice. Naturally, he was unsettled. One case of fire is one too many but two times?! My grandfather consulted an astrologer, a standard practice in those days, and the astrologer advised him not to build any more brick and mortar homes. So instead of building a big brick and mortar home, he built a cluster of small homes with wood and bamboo. Even before it became cool, my grandfather went green, and after that, no more fires in homes were reported.

No wonder Indians consult astrologers!

I also went to see an astrologer once. That was after I graduated from Engineering University; I started applying to American colleges for graduate programs. I was hopeful at first but then I started getting rejection letters and all my optimism was marred. There were a few colleges that I had yet to hear from, so the superstitious gene in my system kicked in. I decided to consult the astrologer. The meeting was probably the most anticlimactic consultation I have ever had in my life. He just said "you will go," and that was it. He did not say where I would go and his appearance did not encourage further queries. I paid him the fee and two years later I was in Detroit.

He said what I wanted to hear; people are not going to give him money just to hear the bad news. Then, some do this as a hobby and do not charge you money. But be careful if you want to go to them; you might end up getting more than you asked for. You may find yourself in a position of distaste because they might give you the "bad news" (the truth).

HOLY MATRIMONY

Since we are on the topic of fortune-telling, did I ever tell you the tale of how the marriage of your grandparents came to be?

It was in 1926, the time when India was British Raj. My father was a young man studying in Kolkata. He used to go to Darjeeling in the summer. During one of these visits, my father was spotted by a man. He was my mother's eldest sister Tahsina's husband Aminul Huq who also happened to be there for some reason. When he saw my father playing tennis, he said to himself,

"That looks like a fine young man. Maybe I should go over there and introduce myself to him. And if he turns out to be as good of a man as he seems, maybe I can play a matchmaker and set him up with my sister-in-law (my mother)."

They had a conversation man-to-man, my father and my uncle; the conversation soon advanced into an invitation for my father to visit my uncle back in Kolkata. They became close in no time. I have not seen him but my mother told us he was a wonderful person, affectionate and caring. My Aunt Tahsina was a loving and tenderhearted person.

My uncle was a great guy. He told my father that his sister-in-law (my mother) was a splendid cook, which was untrue at the time. However, my mother did become a great cook later. He also informed my father that my mother had read many books, which, again, was not true at the time. He was just trying to impress my father and set things in motion with a little nudge. After all, they did not have Tinder and all these on-line matrimonial services in those days! When both concerned parties expressed their interest in each other (thanks to my uncle!) and when the marriage was settled, my uncle brought a lot of books to my mother and told her to read fast.

As you might have already gathered, in those days girls were married off at an early age. If a girl had passed matriculation, tenth grade, she was already a celebrity. People would come to congratulate her for passing her matriculation, and under the cloak of compliments, some would pull her legs about marriage. My mother was no exception. She was also married at a young age.

From a cook who brewed magic with her fingers and a person who could peer through your soul all the while maintaining silence, did my uncle lie about my mother's talents? Did he exaggerate her abilities? Or was he merely speaking of my mother's latent gifts which were to unravel in the days that lay ahead of her? My uncle might not have known it but he was the real astrologer...

My third uncle Mahtab Uddin Chowdhury was already running the affairs of the family estate when my parents were to get married. He was a man of few words, quite reserved, and understood the affairs of the estate. People respected and feared him, which is why my grandfather realized that he was the natural candidate for succession and bequeathed him the responsibility of handling the estate.

When the discussion about the prospect of my parents' matrimony was getting serious, he came to meet my mother and offer his blessings (and approval). He asked my mother a few questions, like if she knew how to cook, standard questions in those days. She did not know cooking at the time.

She learned cooking later. And she probably used to sing by herself as many of us do.

Here is an interesting bit though. After the barrage of questions had ended, my uncle checked underneath my mother's feet (with her permission, of course!) Don't ask me why; I have found some of these "rituals" equally as bizarre as they appear to you while you read this account. I always conclude with the same thought on this part: "They were getting married. It was not like she was joining the army!"

Then again marriages are nothing short of war, I guess.

Afterward, my mother was asked to walk a few steps. My mother complied. In those days, a prospective bride would be asked to walk a few steps. They wanted to see how gracefully a girl could walk. The graceful walk the vital test for any woman! Not very original really, such tests, since these had been set up generations before my mother. Parents knew about these tests obviously, so they would advise their daughters not to walk too fast and flunk the test. I am sure this test is not issued to a prospective bride anymore – times have changed. Today's women do not have the time to prove if they are ladylike with a graceful walk; they have buses to catch and deadlines to meet. Nevertheless, my uncle was satisfied. He gifted my mother a tiara with precious stones on it – a customary gift in the first maiden meeting. He asked my aunt to pierce my mother's nose (another custom before marriage). A diamond would be parked on that spot, so my mother pierced her nose.

She gave away all her jewelry to all her children. Some was lost, and some was stolen. She had saved one of the necklaces that my father had given her. The necklace had been passed down. And we will pass this necklace on to Aneesa.

Since we are on unique marriage rituals, a week before the wedding my mother was confined in a room. No one was allowed to enter her room except very few close family members. No one, other than these members, was to see her. Food was delivered to her room. The idea of premarital confinement was on the premise of an old belief; they said the bride would look radiant on her wedding day... and radiant did my mother look.

And something fascinating happened weeks before the wedding. One of my aunts had an extra toe on her foot. This sixth toe had become somewhat of a crisis for the folks back home. People in those times worried about the most extraneous of things; things that we wouldn't bother about at all. So, they thought that since my mother was a city girl, she might get a negative impression when she sees my aunt's six toes. Hence, they did what seemed to be an obvious solution to them.

They called in the "experts" who armed themselves with probably something sharp from the kitchen and, just like that, the extra toe that made my aunt's anatomy a little unusual was severed off (without anesthesia, of course). My father was in Kolkata at the time and was not aware of the appalling episode that was taking place back home. Naturally, my aunt fainted once she saw blood gushing out of her amputated toe. The "accursed" toe was apprehended in an article of scrapped clothing and then buried in a hole dug outside the house. But fortunately, my aunt recovered well. No infection was reported. And she was now normal like the rest of the crowd.

It is customary in some parts of India and Bangladesh for one to bow and touch the feet of the elders for their blessings. After the wedding, when my mother arrived at her new address and met the elders of the family, she similarly asked for their blessings. My aunt happened to be one of these elders (yes, the very aunt with the severed toe). And my mother noticed nothing unusual there. The "surgeon" had done a good job. Five toes on each foot. She had no idea what they had done to this poor woman.

People came and ate for a month in celebration of my parents' wedding. The kitchen stove was working overtime and burning continuously. My mother thought the whole scene was out of the ordinary. She hailed from a small family and had never experienced anything like it. She mused that these people would run out of money soon, and they did... eventually.

My grandmother was, I guess, germophobic; she had a habit of washing everything. Everything looked dirty to her. As soon as my mother set aside her saree, shoes, and bag from the wedding, my grandmother gave them a good wash. And my mother could not wear or use them anymore. So, one of the first lessons was learned, and subsequently, my mother used to keep her belongings out of her mother-in-law's sight and always locked in.

When my mother was about thirteen years old and was living with her parents in Kolkata around 1920s, the infamous communal riot of India broke out— the disconcerting fracas had evolved into cancerous skirmishes which grew into a complete bloodbath; the groups in question were poaching each other's throats—it was mad. And as things usually develop in such settings, innocent civilians who had no part in the madness were under fire too. And in pursuit of this ignorance, Sikhs were being attacked for bearing semblance to one of the parties. They were beaten and killed.

It was "unbearably horrifying"- those were the words my mother used to define her experience of it. "Cars burnt down... Shops invaded, looted, and left for the ruins... Bodies lying in the streets... The blood ran down the drains as if someone had erroneously dropped a pail of dark red paint in the streams. The gunshots, the screams... the inhumane and barbaric cheers were ear-splitting and the silence that followed foreshadowed the eruption of something more ominous. The smell of rot lingered in every corner of the house. No one could go out for three days." That was the description she provided us when we asked her to elaborate "unbearably horrifying"!

A Sikh family was living downstairs. They had a girl who was my mother's age. She had become good friends with my mother, and then her whole family became close to my mother.

During the riots, it was more sensible to close your doors and windows and block the noise out, but familiar "noises" tend to break down closed doors. A familiar noise imposed upon the attention of my mother on one of these murderous evenings.

It was the Sikh family! She ran downstairs to see if they were all right. A door that was violated led to the mute streets that were painted in red and dusk, and on the threshold of that door, my mother found the head of the family bleeding.

"They are going to come back after regrouping and kill us!"

He embraced my mother and pleaded with her to save his family. My mother took them to an attic and hid them. As they previously presaged, the attackers came back. When they learned of the Sikh family's absence, they asked my grandfather about their whereabouts. My grandfather, however, did not have any knowledge of what had happened to the family; my mother did not inform him that she had hidden them. The aggressors were not as oblivious as my grandfather and had noticed the blood on the stairs up. They pushed their way in despite my grandfather's repudiation of their efforts and found their way into the attic. There were three or four of them, all armed with iron rods (they had been beating their victims to death with those!) At the attic door, they met my mother and quizzed her about the blood stains on her clothes and the blood droplets on the stairs that led to them here. Before my mother could answer them, they spotted the Sikh family through the door behind my mother. The assailants did not require an answer and shoved their way in.

My mother threw herself over the feet of the attackers and begged for mercy. How do you reason with a cold-blooded conscience? I do not know. We must seek the wisdom of selfless maternal disposition for that matter, or to be precise, we must ask my mother how negotiations of such nature turned out! Because the attackers changed their minds (in the face of such bold character perhaps!) and advised her to clean up the blood... and then, they left.

Had you been in your grandmother's position, how would've you felt? Would you have felt ethereal? I probably would be long recovering from the pounding muscle inside my chest even after the attackers had left. My mother said she felt elated that she was able to save this family. The tension evaporating from the attic through the slit of the door was apparent in the beads of sweat that had appeared on the foreheads of every individual there.

Many Sikhs soon left the area after events like these including this family. They came to see my grandfather before they left town. The man thanked my mother for saving their life. My grandfather said, "God saved you. My daughter was merely the means." My grandfather was a man of faith, so he gave credit where credit was due. Besides, people of the East do not exactly make heroes. It is considered impolite.

FATHER

Your grandfather's academic journey began at the esteemed St. Xavier's College located in Kolkata, India. After successfully obtaining his degree from Kolkata University, he had aspirations of furthering his education by studying law in the UK. However, life had other plans for him. A disagreement arose among my uncles, leading to the division of the family's estate among the four brothers. Out of his brothers, my father was the youngest. He, as a result of this unexpected turn of events, was forced to abandon his plans of studying abroad and stay behind to manage his share of the divided estate. It is worth mentioning that at this point, your grandparents were already married.

My uncle (yes, the very one who had appraised my mother before giving his blessings for their marriage) was running the estate before the great fallout. My mother's parents were most disappointed when they learned that their son-in-law was going to pursue his father's "line of work." They said, "Oh Lord, our daughter will be living in a village." Who could blame them? It wasn't exactly the upgrade they had hoped for their daughter! Parents do want the best for their children. Nevertheless, they eventually got accustomed to the scene because even though my mother lived in a village, there was never a dull moment. She was surrounded by people. My uncles' family lived side by side. My parents traveled extensively to all the nice places in India. I guess then my father's parents-in-law understood that what made my mother happy was the best alternative for her.

The year 1947 marked a significant change in the political landscape of India with the British departing the country and the creation of East Pakistan (now Bangladesh). This resulted in many of my father's most cherished places falling on the Indian side of the border, including Kolkata, Agra, Delhi, Darjeeling, Simla, and many others. This meant that he could no longer visit these places which caused him a great deal of grief. Among all the cities he was unable to visit, Kolkata held a special place in his heart. He had spent a significant amount of time there and attended college in this place. He also met my mother there, and the two of them frequently went to the cinema. He used to visit poets and writers of the day, making many wonderful memories. The fact that he could no longer revisit these places and these memories was hard for him to accept; it was hard for many others who were against the Partition. As soon as the British announced that they were going to leave India and India will be partitioned, all hell broke loose. Indians started to kill each other. A million perished during the Partition of India in communal riots. A river of blood flowed.

My father's passion was literature and music.

Your grandfather was a man who was deeply passionate about the art of poetry, had a great love for singing, and was quite the individual. As many Bengalis do, he had a particular fondness for both poetry and singing. Bengalis love poetry, and politics; however your grandfather loved poetry, he found little interest in politics. He would often give singing lessons to members of the family, including my sister. Unfortunately, it soon became clear that my sister was not going to become the budding singer he had hoped for and as a result, the conclusion of the singing lessons was abruptly drawn. Despite this setback, my father's passion for poetry and singing remained undiminished.

My father had a stutter, but when he sang, it was as if a different person had taken over—the stutter would completely disappear. He had a great admiration for those who could write or sing. Unfortunately, none of us in the family became a singer or became writers ourselves. Despite this, I will always remember how singing seemed to bring him a sense of peace and freedom from everything that did not fall into place for him, including the challenge he had with speech. It probably served him as a small but powerful reminder of the transformative power of music.

As time passed, my father gradually gave up many of the hobbies and interests that he had pursued in his early years. He stopped writing poetry, singing, playing tennis, and photography. Raising twelve children must have weighed on him heavily.

In those days in India, a person's worth was often determined by their ability to write. Kolkata was the intellectual center of the country and was home to a myriad of great poets, writers, and men and women of ideas. During British India, countless Indians placed a high value on being able to speak and write perfect English, and your grandfather was no exception. Despite the demands of raising a large family and the pressure to conform to societal expectations, my father never lost his love for learning and continued to strive for intellectual growth throughout his life.

And he exercised his taste in art and literature in his own space. He had a big library, a reflection of his love for literature and art. Yes, the imagery of his library in your head isn't too far off the mark! Vinyl upholstered, polished, wooden chairs and a reading table of the same dark brown finish in the center of shelves of books. All these modern masterpieces were accompanied by other significant works by artists of my father's time in sizes smaller than the originals. He had a collection of hard-bound books on those shelves; I can still sense how the covers felt to the touch of my hand—a memento of something priceless. The books on the shelves were his pride and joy, each one carefully selected and purchased. My father spared no expense to quench his thirst for good literature. The books arrived from the printing circles of Kolkata and later from Dhaka on the weekly train. He must have read each book ten times over.

I wish I could say that my father shared the same affinity with his children that he had with his books. We were not precisely close to my father. Some people are just built differently. Your grandfather wasn't absent in our lives nor did he prioritize other things over us. There is no efficient instruction manual for parenthood. I mean, there probably is but come on, what father or mother would trust some book over their instincts?! In my father's manual, his responsibility was probably to let my mother have complete liberty in bringing us up. That is how "parental instincts" were perhaps formed then. I guess I know where he was coming from. A dozen progenies and men have a notorious reputation for intolerance. Our life revolved around our mother. We were like a solar system—six brothers and six sisters; our mother the sun that glued us together with her gravity.

I remember seeing my father through the window, reading books, surrounded by trees: mango, guava, berries, plums, coconut, and lychee. Their branches leaf through the wind and cast shadows of all shapes as my father flicked through the pages of yet another book. And my mother, in a white saree, would walk into his room holding a freshly made cup of tea. Tranquility ruled the day.

Sometimes, on a test day at school, my father would call me and ask me to bring the question paper. That was one of our more common exchanges. He wanted to know how well I had answered the questions. (As if the test itself was not bad enough!) Then, I had to repeat the same test in front of him which was more daunting than the math teacher's bamboo stick!

Every New Year's morning, he would make us read books. He believed if we had studied on the day of New Year's, we would study the whole year. And we did study the whole year, but it was not my father's superstitions where the credit of our diligence to books was due. His mere presence in the house was enough for us to behave and paste ourselves in front of textbooks. When he was not at home, it was a holiday for us. He was very strict about another thing. As soon as sundown we had to be home. Same rule for us and the herd.

One day, as I returned home from school, my father called out to me. The interactions between your grandfather and his kids were almost as rare as venison in a poor man's kitchen; hence these limited meetings usually meant serious business. So, I walked over to him, feeling a sense of unease and uncertainty. I couldn't help but wonder what might have occurred that would prompt him to summon me. My mind raced with possibilities, trying to anticipate what he might say or what kind of news he might have for me. I stood there, staring at him, as I tried to read his face. My father's expression was serious and I failed to read his thoughts, which made me more anxious. I took a deep breath and waited for him to speak, unsure of what was to come next.

He just said, "Laika is dead. We have buried her in our backyard." In this household, Laika was our beloved pet dog, a happy participant in the family, a loyal friend. Have you heard of a famous dog named Laika? That Laika was sacrificed for man's space exploration in a Soviet spaceship. I was sad that our Laika had died but I was a little surprised to see my father's somber mood. I did not know he cared about Laika that much.

You could say that dogs have been a big part of our family. My uncle had a big black dog; I do not remember his name. Your eldest uncle Khoka would sometimes take this dog and hide him behind a big tree. Just before sunset, when a fox would appear over the very end of the meadow, he would unleash the dog and the dog would run after the fox. He would chase the fox all over the meadow, but the fox would disappear inside a thicket and the dog would bark there for a while before giving up. I don't remember seeing the dog ever getting a hold of a fox; nevertheless, it was a good workout to channel out his "doggy energy!"

We all have frequencies or energies unique to ourselves. And we can sense these, if not recognize them, in the people around us. Our frequencies tune up with these other frequencies to maintain balance. In the absence of just one of the frequencies, the balance is upset.

When I was about nine years old, I went to attend a nearby wedding reception along with other members of the family. My cousin-brother's daughter Khuku had just gotten married. We returned home soon after the evening. When I entered home, I noticed something different. The air felt silent when I entered through the gate. There were members of the family who did not attend the reception, and yet, the silence was eerie.

One of my sisters-in-law took my hand and led me to my father's room. My father was lying on his bed covered with a white sheet, women sat around his bed reading verses from the Holy Quran. He died of a stroke.

And just like that, another frequency in my life waned away. The balance was more upset.

I was young and had my mother, brothers, sisters, friends, nephews, and nieces; I couldn't grasp the severity of the loss then, so I did not miss my father much. The loving and caring family we were helped us through his absence; we always supported each other.

St. Gregory's High School

You have had the opportunity to visit Dhaka, but the metropolis that Dhaka once was is now a distant memory. The city has transformed, a far cry from the sprawling, open spaces, and unrestricted roads that I once knew.

In the Dhaka of my youth, one could easily travel the city while riding a leisurely rickshaw and discovering the city's various areas on their own time. With its imposing skyscrapers and crowded streets, the city is now essentially unrecognizable to me. I am unable to find the areas and monuments that were previously so central to my life. I often feel that I would require a tour guide to direct me down memory lane and point out the way because my school and the places I lived as a child are all but a wisp of my past. I can only hope that by seeking the wisdom of the people who live there, I can recapture the soul of the city I once knew.

Seventh grade. That is when I was acquainted with Dhaka. It was in seventh grade that I moved here. Your second uncle Khaled took the responsibility to enroll me in a school. St.

Gregory's High School, one of old Dhaka's esteemed academic treasures, was an all-in-all Catholic school. The gothic architecture of the school added to its reputation of preserving the pride of one of Dhaka's academic best. As soon as we walked in through those large gates, an aura of seriousness engulfed me. The silence that perspired through the grass as we paced through the courtyard was intimidating, to say the least. Even the Jesus on the cross that hung on the wall in the hallway offered me little comfort.

With every step I gained into the interior of the school, I quickly began to realize that this educational institution was far from the familiar, laid-back school environment that I was accustomed to in my rural village. Unlike the "tranquil" atmosphere of my previous school, where goats leisurely grazed in the front lawn and students could play hooky without consequence, St. Gregory's exuded a more rigid and structured vibe. I could not help but suspect that I would not be able to enjoy the same freedoms and liberties here. With a growing sense of unease, I feared that life at St. Gregory's High School was going to be a significant departure from my past experiences with school.

The white robe seated on the dark brown chair almost extended to the ground; the carrier of the white robe resting his elbows on the chair's arms, all of his fingers interlocked into each other, as his eyes stared at us. I was a little nervous. We were in the headmaster's or principal's office. Headmasters in the States would greet you, welcome you, and assure you of a smooth transition but not the headmasters of Bangladesh then, and certainly not Brother Thomas—the man who sat before me—who engaged in, perhaps, his signature solemn pose which probably feigned deep contemplation to size up every new entry. The silent performance got me even more nervous, but I was accepted to the school.

Once, I spoke during the class: I was immediately served with a detention slip. I had to stay in school for an extra hour. Like I said before, these people meant business, and they didn't look like the types who were interested in making things easy for you. I was not happy about receiving a detention slip but, when I entered the detention room, I was pleased to see I was not going to serve my one-hour sentence alone!

One look around the room and I guessed that they had been giving away these detention slips like Halloween candies. Strict circumstances encourage sneakier approaches after all. And sneakier approaches beget sterner surveillance!

We had to write something like: "I will behave in the classroom" a hundred times; I do not remember the exact words. It didn't take us the whole hour and, living up to the reputation as a band of troublemakers, my new peers and I made productive application of the rest of the detention hour.

Luckily, we had Bengali teachers too. We could talk in their classes, not a problem. Bengali teachers made Catholic schools tolerable. We used to play a sport called "handball."

If I am not mistaken only Catholic schools in Bangladesh had this sport at least when I was there. Even though I was not as crazy about this sport, my peers would line up to play this game. Decades later I saw Aneesa playing this sport in her elementary school in Bakersfield, California.

Father, eldest sister Tahmina left,
second sister Mumtaj on right

eldest sister
Tahmina

second sister
Mumtaj (Hena)

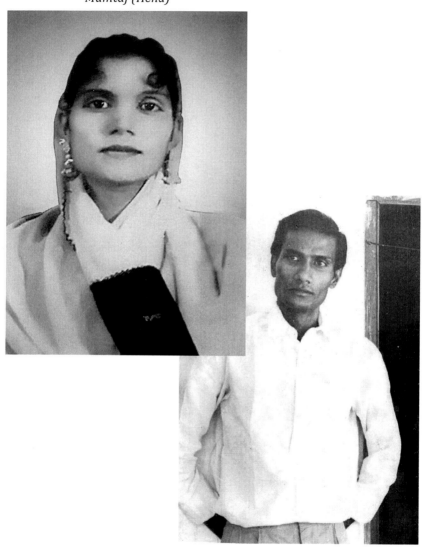

eldest brother
Tahmidur (Khoka)

second brother Khaled (left)
with his friend in Manchester UK

*eldest sister-in-law Anwara
with Tasnuva*

*second sister-in-law
Anwara*

Mother, brother Khaled
in UK

third sister Farida (Tani)
and Saheb Mia

Mother with brother-in-law
Fazle Karim in Iowa

Sisters from left: Shamima, Tahmina,
Liza, Dilruba (Eva)

Brother-in-law Faruquee, Talebur(brother), Shamima(sister)
Saifun(sister-in-law), Tausif (nephew), me

Me, Aneesa,
Ariq

Aneesa winning
Tennis match

x

*Ariq playing in a school
orchestra*

*Padma river
Faisal, Rumana, me, Amirah*

Nephew
Matlubar (Mithu)

Taking a boat ride
in Padma river Bangladesh

*Nephew Tanzib
in his Nairobi office*

*Gang of nephews from left Faisal, Ridwan,
Asaf, Tausif, Ashiq and Lisan*

FAMILY

It was only after I had started living in Dhaka, I realized how quickly the waves of time sweep the past away with changes. When I started to grow my acquaintance with the capital, I could discern the changes that took over in the years between my childhood and my youth. And as far as my apathy for changes was concerned, I was relieved by what I discovered.

Before St. Gregory's happened, before I started being under the care of my brother Khaled and your Aunt Anwara, and when I was a child in Bogulagari who was content playing the role of an average village boy, Dhaka seemed to me like this huge enigma that went on and on for miles; even after being well-versed with the city's history, the vastness rattled me. Of course, once I became accustomed to living there, the feeling eased up and I was able to control the inundation better; consequently, after I arrived in the States, I had to reconsider my view of Dhaka's "vastness." But I do have my reason for my former reservations about Dhaka.

My eldest sister Meena was the first in the family to move here. And after a few of my siblings had left the nest to lodge in Dhaka, the city started to demand the courtesy of the rest of our family. Naturally, we had to visit the city to visit our kin. This was long before I had moved to Dhaka and the mode of reaching Dhaka was not exactly straightforward.

The infrastructure of the country and its future were still being laid out. Nonetheless, our lives could not move as slowly; and as you would observe water making its course through terraneous obstacles, the people of the country, too, had to do with whatever they had.

The path from Bogulagari to Dhaka was not exactly a walk in the park. Every time, we were required to do some serious planning and pull some strenuous stops before we qualified for a welcome by Dhaka. Rangpur district had been in charge of Bogulagari for as long as I can remember. And it took a decent amount of time to reach the Rangpur station from the village by bus. My second eldest sister Hena had settled in Rangpur with her husband; so, we would set our first camp at her place before we boarded the train for our next stop. In the next break of day or darkness, the family would board the train for Fulchori Ferry Ghat. After hastening with our goodbyes to the caterpillar on wheels we would get on the launch in Fulchori which would cruise us around the mighty Jamuna River for about two hours or more before coughing us up to Jamalpur's Bahadurabadh Ferry Ghat where we would be scheduled to board the next caterpillar on wheels. We would end up running to board the train every single time and reserve a good seat, preferably window seats. It made us work for our journey. And then after some hours of trying to catch our breath on the train, we would finally reach... Dhaka.

The journey would take place in reverse when more of us set up shop in Dhaka in the later years. The whole extended family would meet up at the station before the eve of Eid for our holidays and we would run to catch the train to Bahadurabadh Ferry Ghat. (Every day I live, I am more convinced that the engine-man had it in for us!) And then, when we would reach the ferry dock, our faces drenched in sweat and sand, we felt a sense of achievement that was born out of kinfolk sticking together. When we would finally reach our village, we would camp in our rooms and sleep like babies!

And like every fleeting feeling of joy and sorrow, the feeling of achievement didn't last long. Before I was admitted to St. Gregory's, the infrastructure of Bangladesh had finally caught up to the needs of the country's people. Roads were carpeted with asphalt; larger launches were sailing the waters and now we were sailing on board with transports— sometimes on our brother's car, sometimes the public buses on which we traveled. The two stations had finally tied the knot into one and later a stitch of concrete and pillars was drawn over the two ends of River Jamuna; the Jamuna Bridge was complete—a historic moment for Bangladesh. Dhaka was more familiar and closer to me than ever. We grew up and Dhaka did too.

You were not as unfortunate with meeting all your aunts; you did not miss out on their bit of love and affection as you missed out on some of your uncles. You have seen your uncles and aunts. They are loving and caring. I would like to think that you would recall them in the future as fondly as you do now when you talk about them. (Yes, yes... I will ask them to keep the gifts coming for their "demanding" nephew on all the occasions he looks forward to every year.)

All your five uncles have passed away including Zia, Mobinur and Talebur. You knew your Uncle Talebur very well since he lived in Bakersfield. Not so well about your other uncles but you have seen them in Bangladesh. My three sisters have passed away, eldest sister Tahmina (Meena), second sister Mumtaj (Hena) and fourth sister Dilruba (Eva). You are more familiar with my two sisters Liza and Shamima since they live in US. You probably don't remember seeing my third sister Farida (Tani) when you went to Bangladesh many years ago. She lives in our village.

My father was unable to attend any of my brother's weddings. That is the way death works after all. Years before he passed away, he said to my mother,

"It is easy to be a daughter-in-law, but not so easy to be a mother-in-law. You will have six daughters-in-law, they will come from six different families, and they all will have different personalities and temperaments. You will need a lot of patience and understanding."

My mother had patience and was understanding personified! She had a loving relationship with all her daughters-in-law, all six of them.

Our mother was a remarkable person, and it would not be an exaggeration to say that she was the cornerstone of our family. We all felt deeply loved and cared for under her tender care because she never wavered in her kindness, compassion, or patience despite the overwhelming challenge of raising twelve children. She never raised her voice at us let alone expressed indignation of any form. She had a patience envied by heaven. We were all inspired by her grace and serenity in the face of even the deepest sorrows, and her unchanging composure was truly a testament to her inner strength.

In addition to her many wonderful qualities, our mother was also an excellent cook. She approached even the simplest tasks, such as making a poached egg, with the utmost care and attention to detail, always striving to produce a perfect result. Mealtimes were a treasured part of our daily routine because of her compassionate nature and superb cooking abilities, and we will always cherish the memory of those shared moments at the table.

As I recall a nostalgic moment from my past, I recollect a time when my cousin-brother Mahfuz had secured a contract to construct a small bridge in our village. The bridge, probably funded by USAID, was visited by two American consultants who came to inspect its progress. My brother wanted to extend a warm welcome and hospitality to the consultants, so he asked my mother, who was renowned for her culinary skills, if she could prepare a meal for them. She gracefully obliged and cooked her famous roast chicken along with other mouth-watering dishes.

The consultants arrived at our home and were treated to a meal that they would never forget. The flavor, taste, and color of the food left a lasting impression on them as they savored each bite. Before leaving for the city, one of the consultants, with a look of pure delight, turned to my brother and said,

"Mr. Chowdhury, I have never tasted such a delicious chicken in my life."

I doubt that he was exaggerating; the simple words spoken by the consultant were evidence of my mother's unparalleled talent and passion for cooking. She had an unrivaled ability to turn simple ingredients into a masterpiece, and her legacy lives on in the memories of all who have tasted her food.

She was a genius in a craft that she was not native to but learned to wield with time. It was not just her chicken that fetched her reputation for flavors; she had an array of dishes in her arsenal! When "Kaalbaishaki," the April storm, brewed stronger and more forbidding, the ground would be ripe with the heavenly green aroma that completed the pleasant petrichor—a much-sought reward for bearing the heat of summer. The trees that carry the fruits of summer endure the storm's trial. Some stand the test of holding on, and for those that do not, the ground embraced their fall. Young mangoes are the emeralds of summer, but some never make it to adulthood. The resilient wind knocks those green mangoes down during Kaalbaishaki. Children and adults alike would scurry to collect these emeralds as they simultaneously try to save drenching their heads: women would collect their share in the cavity of their scarfs; kids would tuck their t-shirts in their pants and deposit their share of mangoes inside the makeshift "mango slings;" and others just pressed one of their hands against their chests and arrange their mangoes over that hand as they tried to maintain balance. When the storm struck at night, my mother would take a big bucket and run to our backyard as soon as day broke and collect all the mangoes. Then she would make chutneys, pickles, Mango Dal, and other relishes. She was quite resourceful, my mother. That, too, was another of her many qualities that made your grandfather become obsessed with his better half. Indeed, she brought significance as the significant other.

My father's nature of being particularly sensitive made him susceptible to disappointments. Do you remember Uncle Khoka? You last met him back in Dhaka. He was studying in medical school. But less than halfway through his studies, he decided to quit. To say my father was furious at him would be an understatement. After quitting med school, he shifted gears and ventured into the supply business, providing essential goods to the army. One fateful day, he became involved in an argument with a *sepoy*, which escalated to the point where he physically threw a punch at the individual. This resulted in his arrest, causing quite a stir in the family. However, fortunately for us, we had friends in high places and were able to secure his release. You can imagine your grandfather's reaction. First, your uncle quit medical school and now he got arrested for hitting army personnel. As the dynamics of the relationship between the fathers and oldest sons work, the whole scene turned into a father's anguish. Your Uncle Khoka went to live in a town where his chances of meeting our father were less than the chances of meeting Elvis. (After all, numerous Elvis sightings had been reported in various places after he supposedly passed away.) Eventually, your grandfather cooled down, at least to a degree where his temper was bearable. But I am sure my six sisters had an important part to play in that. He was unapologetically partial towards his daughters; they were the apple of his eyes. After all, they were a chip off the old block in terms of our mother, and they comforted him and appeased his anger with his disappointing son.

Oh, how I wish your Uncle Khaled had met you! There was so much he would have loved to teach you and share with you. He passed away five years before you were born. He was the second in the hierarchy among the brothers.

He went to the UK to study Town Planning. I guess Uncle Khaled's academic pursuit made my father happy, and proud even; maybe my father was able to live his dream of walking the lanes of England through my brother's achievements. I am sure his achievements were the balm your grandfather needed to forget disappointment with Uncle Khoka.

Six months after your Uncle Khaled's return from England, my father passed away. My brother practically took over our responsibilities. Three of my brothers, including myself, stayed in his home; he looked after me when I moved in with him to further my education. He also took care of two of our sisters. Your other uncles and aunts also cared for us. All your uncles and aunts carried out their duties with responsibility, with a great deal of love, and with affection. It is just that your Uncle Khaled and your Aunt Anwara went the extra mile and always wanted to share the responsibilities. We were lucky and happy.

Our house was like a hotel. People would come and leave unannounced. Some would stay for a while, some would stay for weeks, and others would go on to stay for years. Your aunt must have made a million cups of tea. There is that thing about tea in this part of the world: when people come over just for a chat, it is never just the tea! It must be accompanied by snacks, at least of one kind. Your aunt never complained. She enjoys having people visit.

Your Uncle Khaled moved to the UK in the later part of his life. Then we stayed with your eldest Uncle Khoka and my eldest sister-in-law Anwara. Yes, she had the same name as my second sister-in-law. As I have said before we are a loving and caring family, always looking after each other. Sadly, both your Uncle Khoka and Aunt Anwara passed away, your Uncle Khoka in 2006 and Aunt Anwara in 2020.

When your Uncle Khaled passed away in 1991 in Coventry, UK, your grandmother said he was a banyan tree who gave us shade. Very true. He was my mother's favorite son. He was everybody's favorite. Our family was never the same after he passed away.

Some years after your Uncle Khaled's death, his only son Tanzib was killed in an automobile accident in Kenya along with his seven-year-old son Zayan—two precious lives lost in a blink, devastating our family. Tanzib was Oxford-educated with a great job at the UN, an all-round sportsman and rugby player, greatly talented at art, and a perfect gentleman. You might remember that your Aunt Liza, Shafi and I visited his wife Rumana, and two of their surviving boys, Jadyn and Aeson, in Kenya. We had a wonderful time in Kenya.

My third uncle Mahtab Chowdhury was an individual of great toughness and strength, possessing a resolute and determined character. He exhibited a thorough comprehension of the intricate and complex affairs of the estate, demonstrating exceptional acumen in managing the various responsibilities of the family. It was this competence and proficiency that made him worthy of being entrusted with the crucial and weighty responsibility of overseeing and ensuring the smooth functioning of the family affairs. And as you might recall from his first encounter with my mother, he was peculiarly strange by present-day standards. Aside from being tough, he was peculiar about something else too.

The Indian subcontinent, comprising India, Bangladesh, and Pakistan, is widely renowned for its profound and intrinsic spiritual legacy. Through the ages, this region has been the birthplace and home to countless spiritual figures, both men and women, hailing from a diverse array of faiths and traditions. From the ascetic Sadhus and Sannyasi, to the enlightened Yogis, the wise Rishi and Maha Rishi, the Vairagi and Bhagwans, the revered Gurus and Fakirs, the mystical Sufis and Pir, the exalted Awliya and Dervishes, the venerated Hazrats and Sheiks, and a host of other ascetics, all of whom have embarked on the quest for the ultimate truth, whatever that may be.

This spiritual lineage can be traced back through the recorded history of India, and beyond, where even Buddhist ascetics were inspired to seek the path of renunciation, transcend all earthly desires, and attain the elusive nirvana. And of course, the naked ascetics (like Calanus) trying to be pure and holy. I must confess that I never have attempted to follow in their footsteps, as the idea of extinguishing all earthly desires proved to be incompatible with my earthly sentiments.

From devout spiritualists to self-professed pseudo-spiritualists, this sub-continent has them all. It is also a place crawling with astrologers, fortune tellers, palm readers, cosmic chart readers, and the rest. They claim to have unlocked the secrets of the universe.

It is not uncommon for people in this part of the world to seek the counsel of such individuals when embarking on a journey, selecting an auspicious date for a wedding, or making any other significant life decision. The belief in the power of these divinatory practices runs deep in the cultural fabric of the region and has been passed down through generations. I must confess that my uncle outshines in this regard—or rather, in the realm of pseudo-spirituality.

My uncle had a jeep, a symbol of status and privilege. He was the "Shaheb," (boss) the only guy who owned an automobile in the area at the time. When people would hear his jeep coming, all the bull carts would clear and make way for him.

He used to perform a ritual before he would travel. To begin this ritual, my uncle would sit down in a chair, while his trusty assistant stood guard to ensure that no one passed between him and the jeep, as it was considered to bring bad luck. My uncle would then proceed to alternate blocking one nostril at a time, blowing forcefully to feel the strength of the air coming out of each nostril. This act of divination held great significance for him, as it determined the foot with which he would take his first step towards the jeep. If his right nostril blew out more air, then he would take his first step with his right foot, and conversely, if his left nostril produced more air, he would begin his journey with his left foot. Only after completing this ritual would he confidently stride toward his prized possession, ready to embark on his journey with a sense of finality and grit.

I know what you are thinking. Just like you, I too, have wondered at times where he picked up this odd habit from and I came to the following conclusion. Some "wise" guy must have told him that he needed to do this every time he traveled to fend off any bad luck, and whatever business matter he was going for would come to fruition. By the grace of good fortune, and, thanks to his "stars" (I think throwing in a bit of pseudo-spiritualistic pun makes more sense while we are on the subject), he never had an accident! With every successful journey, his faith in the ritual only grew. So, you take that as the only explanation behind his superstitions because I am none the wiser!

Batu was the driver of the jeep. In countries like Bangladesh and India, most people would hire someone to drive an automobile. He was a character, to say the least. He possessed a great sense of humor, always chewing betel leaves, and was always able to lighten the mood with his jokes and anecdotes. Batu eventually transitioned from driving the jeep to piloting a bus. I had the opportunity to ride in Batu's bus on numerous occasions. The experiences on his bus have made their mark on my memory and are making their way into this letter that I write to you for various reasons; one of the reasons being that the ride on his bus was not without its fair share of mechanical difficulties.

One persistent issue was the radiator which seemed to have a penchant for leaking at the most inopportune moments. In fact, on an eighteen-mile journey from our home to the nearest town, Batu would have to make no less than three stops to replenish the coolant. His assistant would hastily grab a large bucket and sprint towards the nearest pond, where he would scoop up dirty water to pour into the radiator. It was clear that whoever designed this bus had envisioned that it would undergo severe abuse someday and thus had made it accordingly robust. Another persistent issue with the bus was the hand gear which would frequently become stuck, leaving Batu to struggle with changing gears.

Lastly, the brakes of the bus: I often deliberated if the bus was sentient because of these brakes! The braking system of Batu's bus was not like the typical brakes that we are accustomed to. Whenever he would apply the brakes, the bus would not immediately come to a halt but rather continued to move forward, leaving me with a feeling of unease. How many times was I sure he was going to hit the rickshaw in front of him, but he never did? Despite my apprehension, Batu's driving skills were exceptional as he was able to expertly navigate through the chaotic and bustling streets of the town filled with all sorts of vehicles and pedestrians of varying speeds and attitudes. I often found myself on the edge of my seat, as he narrowly avoided collisions with rickshaws, bikes, motorbikes, bull carts, pushcarts, pedestrians, and other hitches, demonstrating his adeptness in maneuvering the vehicle. It is quite remarkable to contrast this with the spacious and less crowded streets of Bakersfield, where accidents seem to occur all too frequently. Perhaps the bus did have a mind of its own and perhaps Batu understood it; hence, they were in perfect sync! Despite these setbacks, Batu always maintained his cheerful composure, and his infectious laughter could be heard above the clamor of the bus—another reason why I remember him.

I feel compelled to emphasize my Uncle Mahtab's resolve as I write these lines. I do not doubt that you have already started to appreciate the firmness of his convictions which were unshakeable as if they had been set in stone. This quality of his personality was omnipresent, and it pervaded all aspects of his life, from his responsibility as a caregiver to his responsibilities as a brother, as a responsible brother-in-law, and, most significantly, as a father to his children.

Indeed, as a conscientious father, my uncle recognized the significance of maintaining a watchful eye on his sons, especially given that Mozu, his son, was now pursuing further studies in a nearby town after completing his matriculation at

10th grade. Being the responsible and attentive father he was, my uncle considered his protective nature of paramount importance in the upbringing of his son, and he made it a point to visit Mozu, to "offer guidance" and ensure that his son was on the right track. My uncle, thus, was what you could call an advocate of tough love. And so, the unwavering determination and firmness of his personality were reflected in his role as a father.

Sometimes I wonder if I should have been more inspired by my uncle during your school days and "offered you my guidance" from time to time.

As it happened, one afternoon, my uncle decided to drop by to meet Mozu on the way back from the business he was in town for. He drove to Mozu's hostel but found out that Mozu was not there. Someone over at the hostel informed my uncle that Mozu had gone to see a movie. A high school kid went to see a movie—an unforgivable transgression... to my uncle.

To him, the act of skipping classes and indulging in such pastimes was a grave offense that could lead his son astray. He firmly believed that discipline was the cornerstone of a successful life and refused to compromise on his principles. His no-nonsense approach and strict demeanor were the hallmarks of his parenting style, and he was not one to be lenient when it came to discipline. The mere thought of his son wasting his precious time on trivial pursuits was enough to set off a tempest of emotions within him, ranging from disappointment to unbridled fury. Driven by his unwavering commitment to his principles, my uncle resolved to confront Mozu and teach him a lesson that he would never forget.

Mozu's level of enjoyment for the film was nothing short of absolute. My cousin-brother was so captivated by the movie that he indulged himself fully, watching it three times back-to-back! It was a time when cinematic experiences were rare treats that presented themselves only once in a blue moon. This was during the 1950s. News of a new movie release would spread like wildfire through the grapevine, and individuals would mark their mental calendars in anticipation. The excitement for a new movie was almost tangible, and the demand for it was high. As expected, wherever there is a demand, suppliers are bound to crop up and fulfill the need. It was not uncommon for individuals to procure tickets from black marketeers at exorbitant prices, paying up to three times the regular ticket cost. These marketers played hard to get. First, one had to find these guys. They would be lurking in an alley behind the theater hall with the worst display of nonchalance; when one would walk into that alley, they would disregard the new presence. One had to "coax" them to start talking—the lengths people had to go to watch movies!

Following the conclusion of the final screening at midnight, Mozu emerged from the cinema and was taken aback by what he saw. His father's jeep was parked right in front of him, causing him to freeze in his tracks as his heart sank with trepidation, and the ground underneath him started to slip away. During those times, it was the standard punishment for a "serious offense" such as a high school kid attending a movie to be met with physical chastisement, typically a roughing up. However, in a surprising turn of events, my uncle did not resort to such measures. Instead, he escorted his son back to the hostel and instructed him to pack up his belongings, including the mattresses and pillows. My cousin-brother complied without question.

In moments like the one Mozu found himself in, it would be considered utterly impertinent and audacious to question one's father's authority. Even if the circumstances were different and in his favor, Mozu would not dare to challenge his father's commands. It was a cultural norm for a son to never disobey his father; a father held supreme power in the family hierarchy. For instance, a son may fall head over heels in love with a girl, but that was deemed irrelevant as the father would ultimately decide who his son would marry. While the young man may only have eyes for the girl, the father would have his sights set on a broader landscape. The son was expected to conduct himself with the utmost respect and reverence towards his father, and making eye contact while being spoken to was considered disrespectful. Instead, he was to lower his gaze in deference to his father's authority.

(Yes, you too lower your gaze when I speak to you but that is because you are looking at your iPhone!) My uncle brought Mozu home and never returned the kid back to school.

It is fate, it is "Maktoob." This is what could be invoked to explain the events that transpired in Mozu's life. When my uncle brought him home and refused to let him return to school, the only consoling conclusion to be drawn was that it was written in the stars that Mozu's education would come to an abrupt halt. Everybody, including my father, pleaded with my uncle to send the kid back to school but they were only flogging a dead horse. He stood there like an immovable mountain. Sentencing had been carried out and nothing could change that. It was as though the universe had orchestrated events to fall into place in such a way that Mozu's destiny would be shaped in this manner. The grand scheme of things, it seemed, was of greater importance than Mozu's aspirations. Indeed, the forces of the universe could be unforgiving and indifferent to the human experience. Heaven is indifferent; she does not care who gets hurt, whose dream gets shattered, and who gets thrown out of his orbit. She will do what she wants to do to maintain her grand scheme of things.

Mozu found himself sitting at home, at a loss for what to do with his life. Eventually, he took up a teaching job in a school in the area, dedicating himself wholeheartedly to the noble profession. Tragically, he passed away at a young age, leaving behind a legacy of service and dedication. He passed away from heart failure. It was a bitter pill to swallow that life is not always fair, and it is even harder to accept that good people often did not live long, while despots and troublemakers seemed to thrive. Despite the setbacks and hardships, Mozu remained a shining example of human goodness and dedication to the betterment of society. My uncle ended his education after 10th grade, and yet he dedicated his life to educating others; he gave back to the universe instead of trying to take from it and left behind a legacy of kindness and wisdom that would be remembered for years to come.

Toward the end of his life, my uncle experienced a transformative realization. He became aware of the mistakes he had made in his past and the harm he had caused to his relations with others. It was a humbling moment for him, a moment that showcased his vulnerability and humility. A tough guy like him—that was quite a transformation! By that time, many had passed away including your grandfather and the people he had had a conflict with.

It is often the case that people come to realize the errors of their ways only after the damage has already been done. Man's ego is the cause of all the woes of the world, a fact that my uncle's journey toward redemption highlighted. I would like to think that confronting his shortcomings in his later years allowed him to leave this world with a sense of peace and closure.

FIREFLIES

Longevity has its rewards, but longevity can also be punishing; something my mother would have attested to had she been around now. She had been a witness to many pivotal moments in our family's history—some joyous and others tragic—during her eighty-five years on Earth. My father passed away at sixty-two. My father was present at the wedding of only my three of sisters and my mother has seen the wedding of her grandchildren. She visited America and England. My brother Khaled took her to all the nice places in England. My father would have loved to see those places – those were her rewards for being blessed with thirty-five years more than my father, but I am sure she would have liked to share these moments with my father by her side.

And she also had to witness many tragic events in our family. She had to see the passing away of her brothers and sisters, my brother-in-law, and my sister-in-law. Her beloved brother drew his last breath in her arms. She had to endure the passing away of her cherished son, your Uncle Khaled. She said that when my father died it was hard on her, but when

133

my brother died it tore her inside apart. She understood that life's fiery wind comes at us all, and we have no choice but to bear them; she did bear quite a few of them. That was the cost she had to endure for living thirty-five years longer than my father did.

The passing of my beloved mother was only the beginning of a series of heartbreaking events that followed, which I am grateful she did not have to endure. It was as if fate had dealt us an unrelenting series of blows, one after another. Yet, even in the face of such adversity, my mother's legacy continues to live on. News of her passing quickly spread throughout our village, and a deep sadness descended upon our community. She came to live in our village at a young age; my mother had become a beloved member of the village, always there to share in the joys and sorrows of the people she had come to call family.

Despite the villagers' wishes for my mother to be buried within the village, she expressed her desire to be laid to rest near your Uncle Khaled. He had passed away just five years prior, and my mother's final wish was to be buried close to her son; she found comfort in the thought of being reunited with the son who would look after her even in the afterlife. We honored her wishes, and she was buried in a peaceful cemetery in Dhaka, surrounded by her sons, daughter, grandson, great-grandson, son-in-law, and countless other family members whom she had practically grown up with.

When I visit Bangladesh and go to the cemetery, a flood of memories washes over me. So many loved ones, including my mother, lay there, resting in eternal peace. I find myself reminiscing about the days when everyone was alive and life was filled with joy and laughter. I have my deepest sympathy for those who have lost their mothers at young ages. An irreversible loss.

Today, when I go to my village, I find some lingering parts of peace there—part or whole, it is a sense of peace that I am accustomed to. And when I leave my village, I leave with a longing for more. Despite the inevitable changes that have occurred over the years, there is a certain comfort in knowing that some things remain constant.

My third sister Farida (Tani) lives there with her special needs daughter Mitu. My cousin-brother's children and your aunt are neighbors. They tend to each other. It is always heartwarming to see how the bond between our families has remained strong over the years. When I am there, they make meals for me. Even though my sister has become a little frail with age, she gets up early in the morning and brings me a cup of tea and cookies.

The village has changed a lot. Many of the trees I grew up with are gone. With a sigh, every time I am there, I cannot help but wish the village had remained the same. But that is the conundrum; when you return to a place that you had left behind many years ago, how do you expect it to remain unchanged? People change and places change and over time the initial emotional connection that links us to these people and places changes as well.

When I leave the peaceful embrace of Bogulagari, a sense of sadness envelops me like a thick fog. The memories of my childhood spent here with my beloved mother are etched deep in my heart, and the love she showered on this land and its people still lingers in the air like a sweet fragrance. My mother is not here but her presence, and her love is.

Tani and my other sisters have always reminded me of my mother in some way as they have shared the different traits of my mother and passed them on to their children. As I witness Tani's daily life with her special needs daughter, a deep sense of sorrow mixed with helplessness envelops me. Tani's young age was robbed of her by fate, leaving her to shoulder the responsibilities of widowhood and parenthood all alone. Despite her frail health and advancing age, she self-lessly tends to her daughter's needs, day in and day out, with no respite in sight. She is my mother's resilience personified and amplified.

The pang of regret does not take long to set in once I have overcome the satisfaction of touching my nostalgia. The village that I grew up in has undergone a significant trans-formation since I left. I cannot help but feel a longing for the way things used to be. The trees that once adorned the village streets, casting their shade upon us as we went about our daily lives, have all but disappeared. I long for the days when I could wander through the village and feel the same warmth and familiarity that I did as a child. It is a strange feeling to return to a place you once called home, only to find that it no longer feels like home. The people I once knew have grown old, some have left us, and some have undergone similar changes to that of the surroundings they live in. I recognize their faces but I don't know who they are anymore.

Even the emotional connection that I once had to the village seems to have faded somewhat. One of my fondest memories of the village was the sight of fireflies lighting up our backyard on a summer evening. It was a magical sight to behold, and I wonder if it still exists. Perhaps they have been driven away by the sense of loss of their home like me, or perhaps they too visit their old home from time to time when they are at a loss of direction and need to rewire their compasses. But with the changes that have taken place in the village, it is hard to imagine that the fireflies still make an appearance.

In my childhood, we had a Kadamba tree. The tree would be covered with white flowers during the monsoon. Today the tree does not exist. The palmyra tree is dying. Weaver's nests do not hang from the tree anymore. The birds are gone. We had a grand and magnificent blackberry tree that stood tall in our home. Its fruits were so succulent and juicy that they resembled grapes, with a luscious purple interior. But what made that tree truly special were the bees that made their home on a high branch every year. The buzzing sound of the bees would resonate through the tree, creating a natural symphony that appealed to our senses. Whenever the honey harvest season arrived, my mother would call upon the local honey experts to collect the golden nectar. With a long ladder in hand, they would carefully ascend to the branch where the hive was located, smoke out the bees, cut the hive, and transfer it to a bucket. The honeycomb nestled within the hive was nothing short of a pure delight. The richness of the honey, the texture of the waxy comb, and the sweet scent it exuded were incomparable. We would dip our fingers into the bucket and scoop out a piece of honeycomb. Delicious! It was a moment of wholesomeness, and it felt like we were experiencing a true gift from nature.

We had a night jasmine tree known as *Shefali* in Bangladesh. The flowers of this tree have orange stems with a very sweet smell. My mother's favorite flower, it would bloom at night and shed flowers at dawn. Every morning a bunch of flowers would be lying on the ground. Girls from the neighborhood would come and collect the flowers to make garlands. We also had a few exotic flowers that I will never know the names of. None exists today. They died of old age and neglect.

We had a plum tree that had died years ago. My mother used to make chutney with the fruits of the tree. But as time passed, the tree withered away and, despite our attempts to revive it, we had to accept that it was no longer alive. It was a heartbreaking decision, but we cut the tree down eventually.

We also had a star-fruit tree. It was a symbol, a star monument of our home. They called our house "The house with the star-fruit tree." Its bountiful fruits attracted many visitors from the village. We would spend our afternoons lounging underneath its shade, sipping on tea, and snacking on treats. The sight of carefree clouds sailing under the blue sky unconcerned about what might have been happening below them was our favorite pastime under the shade of our star-fruit tree. In winter we would kindle a fire underneath it and keep ourselves warm. But alas, as much as we wanted to keep the tree, we could not ignore the fact that insects had caused significant damage to the inside of the tree, making it unsafe to stand. It was a painful realization, and we had to make the difficult decision to cut it down.

As I walk through the familiar paths of my village in the evening now, my eyes search for the once familiar trees that were constant companions during our childhood. The beautiful trees that bloomed in different seasons, with vibrant flowers of vibrant colors that used to be so beautiful to watch, now seem to have disappeared. The trees that once proudly stood tall in the village and whose leaves rustled in the gentle breeze have fallen prey to the hands of those who now plant trees for a quick buck without any regard for their beauty or worth. Trees that now occupy my village have no beauty and bear no flowers or fruits. Trees too have become mechanical. Bees do not come anymore and make hives. Birds do not build their nests. They too have deserted my home like the fireflies, it would seem.

Regardless of the reason, the possibility of the fireflies abandoning the village symbolizes the changes that have taken place in the village. While I may not be able to recapture the same sense of wonder and enchantment that I felt as a child, I am grateful for the memories that I have. The village may have changed, but those memories will always remain a part of me.

FINAL WORDS

In the later part of her life, my mother moved to live with my sisters and brothers in the city. Our home in the village fell into neglect. The trees that encompassed the character of our home also fell into neglect.

Trees have a way of bearing witness to the passage of time, just like the people in our lives. And while we may wish that things could remain the same forever, the reality is that change is inevitable. Sandpapers might be rough and abrasive but you need something rough and abrasive to smooth and polish things. Life uses time like sandpaper. Just as sandpapers are rough and abrasive, they are also essential for smoothing and polishing things to perfection. The roughness and abrasiveness of sandpapers allow us to remove coarse patches and unevenness, just like how the changes brought about by time allow us to smooth out the rough edges in our lives. We grow old and wrinkle but we are smoother with a memory of our raw self with its rough edges.

I construe the idea of phoenix and rebirth as representative of the idea of parents and their children. The phoenix burns out only leaving its ashes behind. The children are the ashes of their parents—they rise and their parents embody their very being.

We, the remaining ashes of our parents, desperately try to hold onto anything we can to preserve the memories of our parents. We are trying to save many of our mother's memories but time is not on our side.

Remember what I said about legacies? How do we find comfort in knowing that some part of us would be present even after time compels us to leave the stage? There's comfort in our desperation because we know comfort follows this desperation. In the ashes of our parents, a weak speck of ember desperately tries to burn. Then it grows and, as more specks of embers are lit, they grow stronger together. You and Aneesa are these embers; you are ready to make your legacies.

In one corner of a deserted Bogulagari, in the yard of the house that was once home to the star-fruit tree, one lychee tree still stands bearing red delicious fruits every year... and it bears witness to the people who once stood under it.

Your Loving Abbu.